Pensions Handbook

planning ahead 1
retirement incon

Ninth (Revised) Edition

Sue Ward

AGE
Concern

BOOKS

Published by Age Concern England
1268 London Road
London SW16 4ER

© 2002 Age Concern England

Ninth edition

First published 1993

Editor Ro Lyon
Production Vinnette Marshall
Designed and typeset by GreenGate Publishing Services, Tonbridge, Kent
Printed in Great Britain by Bell & Bain Ltd, Glasgow

A catalogue record for this book is available from the British Library.

ISBN 0-86242-354-6

Bulk orders
Age Concern England is pleased to offer customised editions of all its titles to UK companies, institutions or other organisations wishing to make a bulk purchase. For further information, please contact the Publishing Department at the address on this page. Tel: 020 8765 7200. Fax: 020 8765 7211. Email: books@ace.org.uk

CONTENTS

ABOUT THE AUTHOR

Sue Ward is a freelance journalist and researcher specialising in pensions and social security matters.

Her publications include: *Essential Guide to Pensions*, Pluto Press, 1992 (third edition); *Women and Personal Pensions* (jointly with Bryn Davies), HMSO for Equal Opportunities Commission, 1992; *Planning your Pension: A TUC guide*, Kogan Page, 2002; and *Changing Direction: Employment options in mid-life*, Age Concern Books, forthcoming (second edition). She is also the author of regular articles in specialist magazines such as *Pensions World* and *Employee Benefits*.

She was a member of the Occupational Pensions Regulatory Authority (Opra) from its setting up in 1996 until April 2002, and is a governor and member of the Council of the Pensions Policy Institute.

ACKNOWLEDGEMENTS

This is the latest edition of a book written originally by Jennie Hawthorne in 1993. Her work on the concept, and the draft, must be fully acknowledged. With changing circumstances in the pensions world, much further work has gone into all the revisions since. I must take full responsibility for any mistakes and errors.

My thanks to Ro Lyon for her excellent editing, and to Richard Holloway, Vinnette Marshall, Jeremy Fennell and other staff at Age Concern.

Over the years the following organisations have given generously of their time, the facts at their disposal and their opinions. All were gratefully received.

Alexander Consulting Group
The Annuity Bureau
Association of British Insurers
Clerical Medical Investment Group Ltd
Department of Social Security (Press Office) – now Department of Work and Pensions
Equal Opportunities Commission
Equitable Life
Financial Services Authority
Fiona Price and Partners
Inland Revenue
Legal and General Insurance (Ron Spill)
London Life Limited
National Association of Pension Funds
Office of the Pensions Advisory Service (OPAS)
Pensions Management Institute
Pensions Ombudsman
Pensions Registry
Pensions World
Transport and General Workers Union (Legal Department)

Sue Ward
July 2002

INTRODUCTION

When we are young, most of us work on the assumption that we are never going to get old. As time goes on, we discover that we are just as likely to get old as anyone else is. So then we begin to think about retirement and what we will have to live on. Most of us then realise that, however much we know about our own jobs and about life in general, we know little or nothing about pensions.

Over the years, many studies have shown that most people are confused by the pensions system, and have very little idea of what income they will have in retirement. However, saving for retirement is more important now than it has ever been, because our generation can expect to live so much longer than generations in the past. The increasing numbers of people who take early retirement are likely to have even more time ahead of them. To make the most of retirement you will need a reasonable income.

People born in the 1940s and 1950s grew up with the expectation that the Welfare State would offer them a pension on retirement that was enough to live on, paid for from National Insurance. Government policies have changed since then, however, and State benefits are nowhere near enough to provide a comfortable retirement. It is becoming increasingly important to have other sources of income apart from the State. The State Basic Pension, and the additional pensions available from the State Earnings-Related Scheme (SERPS), now replaced by the State Second Pension (S2P), are expected to increase only in line with prices. Since earnings on the whole go up faster than that, the income of people relying on these benefits will fall further behind the working population as its standard of living rises. Ultimately, according to the Government's Green Paper on the subject, the Basic and Additional Pensions from the State added together, will be a lower percentage of average earnings than the Basic Pension alone was in 1980. The new S2P offers more than SERPS previously did to the lowest-paid and to carers. Nonetheless, government policy is based on the idea that those who can save for retirement should do so, with the private sector taking on a larger share of pension provision than it does currently.

Extra income for retirement can come from your savings in general, or from a pension. Contributing to a pension scheme is generally the most tax-efficient way of saving for retirement. It also means that once the money is set aside, it is locked away until retirement and you cannot give in to the temptation to spend it on anything else.

The keys to successful retirement provision are:

- increasing the proportion of your current income that you put aside; and
- making sure that the money set aside is working as efficiently as possible for you.

The five ages of pensions

Even 20-year-olds would be wise to think about their pensions from time to time, but it becomes more urgent as you get older. You can divide your adult lifetime roughly into five 'ages' with different issues to think about as you get older:

Under 40 Retirement seems a very long way off and you probably don't think that pensions need concern you yet. However, the earlier you can put money away the better, especially if you are relying on a money-purchase pension arrangement (see page 41). The longer the money is there, the bigger the investment returns it can build up and so the less you have to put in overall. You may be hard-pressed financially, especially if you are bringing up a family, but a pension is a good place in which to put windfalls and lump sums that come your way. If you are lucky enough to be able to join an employer's final earnings pension scheme (see pages 39–41), then the more years you belong, the greater the pension you will build up.

40 to 50 You should definitely be making pension provision for yourself by now; if your employer does not offer a scheme, or if you are self-employed or not earning at all, look at taking out a personal or stakeholder pension. If you already have a pension building up, check the estimates of what you will get and decide whether you should be increasing your contributions. Check also your National Insurance position – if there were earlier gaps in your working life, you may be able to make voluntary contributions to fill them in.

50 to 60 Most employers' pension schemes allow you to retire at any age from 50 onwards. You are also able to draw a personal or stakeholder pension from this age. Often, however, the pension is so much reduced that this is not realistic. Check the position in your own scheme. The employer may be offering a special early retirement package, if it is looking to cut staff. Decide whether it is worth taking this up. You will not be able to draw a State Pension at this stage, however, and other benefits such as Jobseekers' Allowance or Incapacity Benefit may be reduced to take account of your private pension. It is still not too late to increase the percentage that you pay in contributions. It could be worth transferring money from other forms of savings into a pension scheme, so look at your financial position as a whole.

60 to 75 Many employers' pension schemes allow people to retire on a full pension from 60 – check the position in yours. You will usually have a choice of whether to take the maximum amount as a tax-free lump sum, or a smaller lump sum and a larger pension. If you have a personal or stakeholder pension (and some sorts of employers' pensions) you may be able to choose between different sorts of annuity, and whether to take income directly from the fund rather than buying an annuity. Most providers allow you to shop around for the best value annuity (this is called the 'open market option' and is explained on pages 96–97). This can make a very considerable difference to the amount of income you receive, so it is well worth doing. At present, if you are a woman, you will be able to draw State Pension from 60, while a man has to wait until 65. (However, retirement age is due to change, in stages, for women born after 6 April 1950.) If you are still working, you might want to defer the State Pension and build up an increased amount later. You can also continue to pay into a personal or stakeholder pension scheme, up until the age of 75.

75 plus If you have not started drawing on your personal pension yet, or if you have been drawing income directly from the fund, you *must* now do so (although with some employers' pensions you can defer it for longer if you wish). It is still worth checking which annuity provider will give you the best deal by using the open market option.

Women and pensions

Women have some special problems with pensions, so it is even more important to think about them early, and carefully:

- In general, women earn less than men, tend to have gaps in their working lives and therefore a shorter National Insurance record, and tend to live longer, often alone. So women need to take every opportunity to ensure an adequate income in retirement. In the past, the law did not allow people who had no earnings to contribute to a private pension, but since April 2001 this has been allowed, and women who have gaps in their working lives can particularly gain from this.
- Many married women expect to rely at least partially on their husband's pensions. They often also assume that, if anything should happen to their husband, there will be a widow's pension for them. Sadly, many marriages do not last into retirement and the pension position on divorce can be complicated. State widows' pensions have also been reduced, so there will be less to rely on from that source.
- If you are living with someone to whom you are not married, you may regard yourself as being in just the same position but the law does not. Some employers' pension schemes will give the equivalent of a widow's pension to a 'dependant', but

many do not. The State is especially rigorous in demanding a marriage certificate before it will pay out.

- Over the last decade, there has been pressure to treat men and women equally in pension terms. The process has brought advantages for women, but also disadvantages. Younger women (those born after April 1950) will see the age at which they can draw their State Pension rise to 65. Most employers' pension schemes already have equal retirement ages, and often this is 60 for both sexes.

The aim of this book

This book is intended to give you the information you need at the point at which you become concerned about your pension. It is aimed at people of any age, but especially between 40 and 60 or so, whether in a job, self-employed, or not in paid work. We have tried to explain a complicated system in simple terms, but there is bound to be some jargon, and many issues are too detailed to be dealt with in depth. So there is a glossary (from the Plain English Campaign) and a list of addresses for further information at the back. The text also contains reference to other leaflets that are available.

- **Payment rates, and statements about the law, are based on the situation as at 8 April 2002. There may have been later changes, so make sure you have up-to-date information before taking further action. The next edition of this book should be published in September 2003.**

The Department of Social Security (DSS) changed its name in June 2001 to the Department of Work and Pensions (DWP). The name and initials have been changed in this book, but you will find that for some time to come, leaflets and other literature continue to use the old name, as earlier stocks are used up.

In April 2002 the Department for Work and Pensions (DWP) reorganised itself internally. The part of it that deals with State Pensions is now called The Pension Service. There is a phased programme of change, so that by 2004 there will be 26

'Pension Centres' spread across the country, backed up by a local service in social security offices, working in partnership with other local pension-related organisations. To find out who to contact during the interim period, ring your local social security office or, if you have access to the Internet, look under 'Contact us' on the website www.the pensionservice.gov.uk

State Retirement Pensions

Nearly everyone pays National Insurance contributions towards their State Pension at some point in their lives, and most people can expect to receive something from the State when they retire. This chapter looks at the different parts of the State Pension; drawing your pension; and increasing your pension by paying voluntary contributions or deferring drawing it.

HOW THE STATE PENSION WORKS

The State Pension comes in two main parts. There is a flat-rate Basic Pension, and an earnings-related pension on top. Until April 2002, this was called the State Earnings-Related Pension Scheme (SERPS). The name was changed at that point, however, to the State Second Pension (S2P), and the way it was calculated also changed. SERPS benefits already built up have been safeguarded, however.

There is also a small Graduated Pension, if you paid graduated National Insurance contributions between April 1961 and April 1975, and a 'non-contributory' pension for people aged 80 or more. All these are taxable.

If your State pensions and other income do not give you enough to live on, you may be able to claim means-tested Income Support (called the Minimum Income Guarantee (MIG) when it is for pensioners) and both Housing Benefit and Council Tax Benefit as well. These social security benefits are not covered in this book – for further information see the Age Concern annual publication *Your Rights* (see page 167). In October 2003 the MIG will be replaced by the new Pension Credit.

Basic Pension

The State Basic Pension is payable at the same rate to everyone who has reached pension age (currently 60 for women and 65 for men but see the chapter on pensions issues for women for details of the changes in women's retirement age) and meets the National Insurance contribution conditions. The full weekly rates from April 2002 to April 2003 are:

Single person	£75.50
Wife on husband's contributions	£45.20
Married couple on husband's contributions	£120.70
Married couple if both paid full contributions	£151.00

A reduced amount is payable if you do not have a full National Insurance contribution record, as explained on pages 6–8.

The Government announces each November how much the rates will increase the following April. The level of increase depends on the rise in the Retail Prices Index for the year up to the previous September, although this year there has been an above-inflation rise.

State Retirement Pensions for married women

If you are a married woman and you have paid full NI contributions for all of your working life, you should be entitled to a full State Basic Pension when you reach State Pension age. If you have paid full contributions for only part of your working life, you may be entitled to a reduced pension. Any years when you were paying the married woman's reduced-rate contributions (see pages 114–117) do not count towards a pension in your own right.

If you have not paid enough contributions to qualify for a pension in your own right, you will have to rely on your husband's contribution record. You can draw the married woman's pension, currently £45.20 a week, when your husband is 65, provided he does not decide to defer drawing his pension. However, if he does not have a complete contribution record, you too may get less than the full amount.

If the pension based on your own contributions is less than £45.20, it will be made up to a maximum of this amount when your husband draws his pension. If your own pension is more than this, you cannot get any extra pension based on your husband's contributions.

This is because of a general rule within the social security system called the 'overlapping benefits' rule. This rule says that if you have a potential entitlement to two benefits at the same time, you receive only the higher of the two, and not both.

Increases for dependants

Dependent wives

If you are under 60 when your husband draws his pension (at 65 or over), he may be able to claim an increase of £45.20 a week for you. However, he may not be able to receive this increase if you receive another State benefit of £45.20 or more or have earnings of over £53.95 a week, after certain expenses connected with work have been deducted. An occupational or personal pension counts as earnings for this purpose. If you are separated from your husband, he can still claim the increase for you but the earnings limit is £45.20 a week.

If your husband retired before 16 September 1985 and has been receiving an increase in his pension for you since then, a different rule applies. The earnings limit will then be £45.09 a week, and the increase is gradually reduced if you earn more than this.

Once you reach 60, you will qualify for a pension in your own right, on the basis either of your own National Insurance record or your husband's.

Dependent husbands

If your wife is receiving a State Pension, she may be able to get an increase for you if she was receiving an addition for you with Incapacity Benefit immediately before she started drawing her pension. But she will not receive any increase if you have earnings of over £53.95 a week or receive a State Pension or certain other benefits of £45.20 or more.

The dependency rules will be equalised, and the conditions made the same as for dependent wives, at the same time as women's retirement age is increased (see pages 117–118).

Who qualifies for the Basic Pension?

First, you must have reached State Pension age. You then need to claim your pension. About four months before your 60th/65th birthday, you should be sent a retirement pack. If you do not receive a pack, contact the Pension Service yourself. (See page 25 for how to claim by telephone.)

Second, the Pension Service looks back at the records of your National Insurance contributions over the whole of your working life. Before 1975, contributions were made by putting a stamp on a card each week. Since 1975, if you are an employee they have been made through a percentage deduction from your pay, collected via the tax system. Self-employed people pay a flat-rate contribution to the National Insurance Contributions Office (NICO) with an extra earnings-related element payable alongside their tax bill.

To get any State Basic Pension at all, you must, at some point in your working life, have paid *either* 50 weekly NI stamps in the pre-1975 system *or* enough earnings-related NI contributions in any year since 1975 to make it a 'qualifying year'. This is known as the 'first contribution condition'. For the 'second contribution condition', NI credits also count – see below for details of the credits.

To get a full Basic Pension you must have paid or been credited with NI contributions for most of your 'working life', as explained in the next section.

Normally you need to have satisfied the contribution conditions in your own right, but married women, divorcees and widowed people may be able to claim a pension on their spouse's or ex-spouse's contribution records. Pensions for divorced people are explained on pages 130–131 and for widowed people on pages 18–22.

Your working life

Your 'working life' is the period on which your NI contribution
record is based. It normally starts in the tax year during which
you reach 16. It ends with the last full tax year before your
60th (women) or 65th (men) birthday or the last full tax year
before your death (this is important for the calculation of
bereavement benefits). The normal working life is therefore 49
years for a man (16–65) and 44 years for a woman (16–60).
This will change from 2010 onwards for women, and by March
2020 it will also be 49 years for a woman.

Qualifying years

A 'qualifying year' is a tax year in which you have paid (or been
credited with) contributions on sufficient earnings to count
towards your pension record. The rules about what constitutes
a qualifying year have changed a number of times.

Before 1975 working people paid contributions by weekly
stamp, or received credits in certain cases, as explained on page
10. For years up to 1975, all the stamps and credits are added
up and divided by 50, rounding up any that are left over. But
you cannot have more qualifying years worked out in this way
than the number of years in your working life up to April 1975.

Since 1975 contributions have been based on a percentage of
earnings and collected through the tax system. Between 1975
and 1978 a qualifying year was one in which you paid or were
credited with contributions on earnings of at least 50 times the
weekly Lower Earnings Limit. The 'Lower Earnings Limit'
(LEL) is usually around the level of the Basic Pension and is the
minimum level of earnings that qualifies for contributory
benefits. Since 1978, a qualifying year has been one in which
you had earnings of at least 52 times the weekly Lower
Earnings Limit.

If you earn between the LEL and the Earnings Threshold (see
page 8) you will not actually be paying any contributions.
Technically, however, you are counted as if you are doing so,
although at a zero rate, so these weeks qualify for this purpose.

To receive a full Basic Pension, about nine out of every ten years in your working life need to be qualifying years, according to a scale laid down by the DWP.

Length of working life	Number of qualifying years needed for a full Basic Pension
41 years or more	Length of working life minus 5
31–40 years	Length of working life minus 4
21–30 years	Length of working life minus 3
11–20 years	Length of working life minus 2
1–10 years	Length of working life minus 1

If you have fewer qualifying years than this, you will be paid a reduced Basic Pension. The minimum pension actually payable is 25 per cent of the full rate. The table below shows the percentage of the full pension for which you would qualify, assuming your working life is the full 44 years (women) or 49 years (men):

Number of qualifying years	Percentage of the full Basic Pension for which you qualify	
	Women	*Men*
9 or less	0	0
10	26	0
11	29	25
15	39	35
20	52	46
30	77	69
39	100	89
44 or more	100	100

Christine was born on 10 August 1946 and was 16 in 1962. Her working life runs from 6 April 1962 to 5 April 2006, a total of 44 years. To receive a full Basic Pension, she needs 39 or more qualifying years. If she has worked and paid, or been credited with, contributions for only 20 years of her working life, she will receive just over half the Basic Pension.

Home Responsibilities Protection reduces the number of qualifying years for anyone not working because they are looking after a family and is explained on pages 120–123.

National Insurance contributions and credits

There are several different types of NI contribution.

Class 1

Class 1 contributions are paid by employees and their employers. Since April 2000, they have been restructured. There are three important earnings levels. These are:

- the Lower Earnings Limit (LEL)
- the Earnings Threshold (ET)
- the Upper Earnings Limit (UEL)

The table below shows what these are, in weekly, monthly, and annual terms, during 2002–2003:

	LEL	ET	UEL
Weekly	£75	£89	£585
Monthly	£325	£385	£2,535
Annual	£3,900	£4,620	£30,420

The way the system works is:

- If you earn less than the LEL, you do not pay any National Insurance contributions, but neither are you building up a

National Insurance record to help you qualify for National Insurance benefits.

- If your earnings are between the LEL and the ET, you still do not pay any National Insurance, but your earnings above the LEL are counted for NI purposes as if you *are* paying. (Technically, you are considered as paying NI but at a rate of 0 per cent.)

- If you are earning above the ET, but less than the UEL, you pay a percentage of all your earnings above the ET in National Insurance, and all your earnings above the LEL are counted for NI purposes. The percentage you pay depends on whether you are 'contracted in' or 'contracted out' of SERPS via an employer's pension scheme (explained on pages 14–16). If you are not a member of an employer's pension scheme, you pay National Insurance at the contracted-in rate. Those who are contracted in pay 10 per cent, while those who are contracted out pay 8.4 per cent.

- If you are earning more than the UEL, you are treated for NI purposes as if you are only earning the same amount as the UEL (a maximum of £585 a week this tax year). This changes, however, in April 2003, when employees will also start paying a 1 per cent contribution on their earnings above the UEL.

The *employer's* NI contributions start at the ET (£89 a week in 2002–2003) and there is no ceiling on them. The employer's contracted-in rate is 11.8 per cent, while the contracted-out rate is 8.3 per cent (or 10.8 per cent for certain types of employers' schemes). To complicate matters further, contracting out only applies on earnings between the LEL and the UEL.

Reduced-rate contributions for married women are considered on pages 114–117.

Class 2

Class 2 contributions are flat-rate contributions paid by self-employed people (currently £2.00 a week in 2002–2003). They count towards the Basic Pension but not towards S2P.

Self-employed married women who chose to pay reduced-rate contributions when they were available, and have never changed to the full rate, pay no Class 2 contributions.

Class 3

Class 3 contributions are flat-rate voluntary contributions. They are £6.85 a week in 2002–2003. Anyone facing a gap in their contribution record may be able to catch up on missed contributions and protect their pension by paying these, but only for the previous six years. This could cover, for example, a period overseas. The National Insurance Contributions Office (NICO) is supposed to send a Deficiency Notice to all those who have a gap in their contributions, about 18 months after the end of the tax year in which it arose, so that they can decide whether to pay voluntarily to fill in the gap. NICO admits, however, that this does not always happen.

Class 4

Class 4 contributions are paid by self-employed people at a rate of 7 per cent on profits between lower and upper limits (£4,615 and £30,420 in 2002–2003). These contributions do not entitle you to any extra benefit, however.

Credits

Men between the ages of 60 and 65 who do not have any earnings receive 'autocredits' (ie, they are automatically treated as if they have paid NI contributions), unless they are self-employed or are abroad for more than half the year. (This will also apply to women once they have equal State Pension age with men).

Credits can take the place of NI contributions in certain other circumstances also. The main ones are:

- if you are registered for Jobseeker's Allowance and seeking work (so it may be worth registering even if you do not qualify for any benefit);

- if you are unable to work because you are sick or disabled;
- if you are receiving Disabled Person's Tax Credit, or in some cases Working Families' Tax Credit; or
- if you are receiving Invalid Care Allowance.

Check whether you are eligible for any of these credits, or if you qualify for Home Responsibilities Protection (explained on pages 120–123), before spending your own money on Class 3 contributions.

In some cases you may need to write to NICO to claim a credit. Check with the social security office at the time whether this applies to you.

Working abroad

If you work abroad but still officially live in this country, you usually have to pay NI contributions. If you work for a multinational company abroad, it will probably arrange to do this for you. If you are not domiciled here, you will not need to pay UK contributions, but you may be required to contribute to your host country's social security benefit arrangements for benefits there. You can sometimes make voluntary (Class 3) contributions during periods of overseas service, but there are time limits for making them.

Before you go, check with the Pension Service Overseas Branch about the position in the country where you plan to work. There are special arrangements for 'migrant' workers within the European Union and a number of social security treaties with other governments. If for some reason you will not be covered, ask for additional payment from your employer so that you can make private arrangements.

For details of the position regarding State benefits for the country you are going to, write to the Pension Service Overseas Branch at the address on page 161. See Inland Revenue leaflet NI 38 and social security leaflet GL 29.

The State Second Pension (S2P)

The second tier of State retirement provision is now called the State Second Pension (S2P). The previous SERPS pension that you have built up will be safeguarded, so this section explains how both SERPS and S2P work.

Who qualifies?

In order to have any S2P (or SERPS before it) you must be paying Class 1 NI contributions for employees (explained on pages 8–9). You do not build up entitlement during years when you are self-employed and paying Class 2 contributions. Widows and widowers may qualify for SERPS and S2P on their spouse's contributions. It is possible to have some pension from SERPS or S2P, even if you do not qualify for any Basic Pension.

How does S2P work?

Your S2P (and SERPS before it) depends on your 'band earnings' or 'reckonable earnings' during your working life. These are earnings between the Lower and Upper Earnings Limits for each tax year from 1978–79 until the year before you reach pension age. The 2002–2003 weekly limits are £75 and £585. So if you earn £300 per week in 2002–2003, your band earnings will be £300 – £75 = £225.

S2P/SERPS is calculated by first revaluing your band earnings for past years in line with rises in national average earnings, according to an index produced by the DWP. Your band earnings for each year are then added together, and averaged.

The various rates change each year, and may be very different by the time you come to retire. In today's money, however:

- Any employee whose 'band earnings' are less than £10,800 a year but more than the Lower Earnings Limit (£3,900) will be treated under S2P as if their earnings are £10,800.
- Many carers will also be credited in to the scheme as though they had earnings of £10,800 a year.

If you qualify for Invalid Care Allowance (ICA) because you are looking after a person with disabilities, these credits are automatic. However, if you do not get ICA but are looking after someone who receives Attendance Allowance, or if you receive Income Support, without having to sign on as a jobseeker because you are looking after someone with a disability, you can apply for Home Responsibilities Protection (HRP), as explained on pages 120–123.

If you are the 'main payee' for Child Benefit for a child aged 6 or under (a lower age limit than for the State Basic Pension), you will be given HRP automatically.

For more information, see DWP leaflet PM9 (March 2002) *State Pensions for Carers and Parents: Your guide.*

People with disabilities will also be credited for complete years when they were receiving Incapacity Benefit (IB) or Severe Disablement Allowance (SDA), *so long as* they worked and paid Class 1 NI contributions for at least one tenth of their working life.

Calculating S2P

The calculation of S2P for those above the basic level is complex, and it links back to the way SERPS was calculated for years up to April 2002. Originally, the 'band earnings' (explained on page 12) were divided by 80, for anyone who reached pension age before 6 April 1999. If they had contributed to SERPS for the full 20 years, they received the maximum pension of $\frac{20}{80}$ (25 per cent) of their average revalued band earnings. Changes were made to SERPS in 1986 which began to come into effect in 1999–2000. The maximum SERPS Pension of 25 per cent began to be phased down by 0.5 per cent from the tax year 1999–2000, and will reach 20 per cent in 2009–2010.

Under the State Second Pension:

- For earnings between the Lower Earnings Limit and £10,800 a year (whether this is the actual amount of your earnings or the notional amount for the purposes of this calculation), the S2P will build up at double the SERPS rate. Low-paid people will therefore receive considerably more than they would under SERPS.
- For earnings between £10,800 and £24,600, S2P will build up at half the SERPS rate.
- For earnings over £24,600, S2P will build up at the same rate as SERPS.
- People can contract out of S2P into a non-State pension, as they could out of SERPS, with part of their National Insurance contributions going to that other pension instead. Anyone who has contracted out but is earning less than £10,800 in a year will get their non-State pension topped up by a payment of S2P. The contracted-out occupational pensions of people earning up to £24,600 will also be topped up from the State.

After the new system has been running for about five years, there may be another reform to make the S2P largely flat-rate for people below a certain age: the cut-off point is likely to be 45. The Government has said that it will wait and see whether its new stakeholder pensions (explained on pages 92–94) are a success, before moving on to this stage.

Social security leaflet NP 46 on Retirement Pensions gives detailed examples. Look at these if you are interested in seeing how the calculations are done. Alternatively – and more simply – you can find out your current and projected SERPS/S2P entitlement by filling in form BR 19 and sending it to the Retirement Benefits Forecasting Unit, as explained on page 23.

Contracted in or out?

If you are a member of an occupational pension scheme (explained in more detail in the next chapter), you could be either contracted in or contracted out of S2P. If you are contracted in, this means that you pay the full amount of National Insurance contributions, and when you retire you will be paid both an employer's pension and a S2P pension (plus the Basic State Pension in any case as contracting out does not affect it).

Most members of occupational pension schemes, however, are contracted out of S2P. This means that both you and your employer pay lower National Insurance contributions. The difference is called the 'rebate', and is currently 1.6 per cent of 'band earnings' (earnings between the LEL and the UEL, explained on page 9) for the employee. For the employer, the rebate can be either 1 per cent or 3.5 per cent, depending on the sort of scheme it is.

This rebate is intended to cover the costs of the S2P you are foregoing. Since 1997, however, none of the different types of scheme guarantee that you will definitely receive as much as you would have done if you had stayed in SERPS/S2P. That depends on several factors, including your earnings pattern, the quality of the scheme, and in some cases how well the money is invested.

There were, however, a number of guarantees of what pension you would get if you were contracted out before April 1997, and these still exist for the part of your pension that relates to these earlier years:

- Until April 1997, any final earnings pension scheme (explained on pages 39–41) that was contracted out of SERPS had to provide each person with a Guaranteed Minimum Pension (GMP). The GMP was more or less the same as the SERPS pension they had given up, although the way it was calculated was different.
- The GMP was worked out in a different way from SERPS, but to ensure that no-one lost out, the National Insurance system made up any shortfall. So many people, even if they have been contracted out since SERPS started in 1978, have a little bit of SERPS pension to come when they retire.
- The original arrangement, in 1978, was that once the GMP started to be paid the occupational scheme did not have to

increase it at all; the State would do that through giving an increase in the State Retirement Pension. In 1986 this changed, and the employer became responsible for paying the first 3 per cent increase (depending on the rate of inflation) and the State paid the rest.

- In the other sort of contracted-out pension scheme, a money-purchase scheme (COMP), there was not a GMP but there was (and still is) a Protected Rights pension. There was no guarantee of how much this would be, but the State assumed it would be the same as the GMP, made a deduction from your SERPS accordingly, and gave increases in the same way as for the GMP.

So most people retiring today, and in the near future, will have a pension payment from the State that includes some SERPS as well as the Basic Pension. As time goes on, however, this will become less significant because of the way contracting out changed in 1997, under the 1995 Pensions Act.

For pensions built up after April 1997, this Act 'broke the links' between SERPS and a contracted-out scheme. So now if your scheme is contracted out on a salary-related basis, the scheme's actuary has to certify that the scheme will give benefits at least as good as those in a 'reference scheme' laid down by law to at least 90 per cent of the members.

Under the rules for the new S2P, the contracting-out rules stay the same but, for those in occupational pension schemes, earning less than £24,600 (in today's figures), there will be a State Pension 'top-up' to ensure that they do not lose out because of the differences between SERPS and S2P. This will be calculated and paid automatically by the DWP at the time of retirement.

Graduated Pension

As well as the Basic and SERPS/S2P pension, many people coming up to retirement find that they have a small amount of Graduated Pension. This comes from a scheme that lasted from April 1961 to April 1975. It was then frozen until 1978, but since then it has been inflation-proofed at the same rate as the Basic Pension.

The Graduated Pension is based on the number of 'units' paid between 1961 and 1975 and the value of a unit when the pension is claimed. Women get 9.21p per week for every £9 paid, men 9.21p for every £7.50 paid. Most people who receive Graduated Pension get less than £3 a week.

It is possible to qualify for a Graduated Pension even if you have not paid enough contributions to entitle you to the Basic Pension. However, there can be disadvantages in claiming it, as explained on page 28.

While the Graduated Pension scheme was running, there were 'contracting-out' arrangements for people who belonged to their employers' pension schemes. Contact the Pension Schemes Registry (address on page 163) if you have lost touch with your ex-employers and think they may have had a scheme.

Pensions for people over 80

Over-80s Pension

This is a non-contributory Retirement Pension of £45.20 a week for people aged 80 or over who do not qualify for a Retirement Pension. For someone who already gets a Retirement Pension of less than this amount, an Over-80s Pension will be paid to bring their pension up to this level.

To qualify for this pension you have to be living in the UK on the day you become 80 or the date of your claim if this is later, and to have been here for 10 years or more in any 20-year period since your 60th birthday. If you have lived in another European Union country (including Gibraltar), this may help you qualify.

See social security leaflet NP 46.

Age-related additions

Once you reach 80 you receive 25p per week extra with your Retirement Pension. If a husband and wife are both over 80, they each receive the extra amount.

Pensions for widows and widowers

- The rules have changed for people whose spouses die on or after 9 April 2001. This section therefore covers the new arrangements, although people who were widowed in previous years will still receive pensions under the old rules, which are covered briefly at the end.

Bereavement Payment

You will receive a non-taxable single lump sum Bereavement Payment of £2,000, provided that:

- your husband or wife had the right National Insurance contributions in the past (most people will qualify under these conditions); and
- your husband or wife was not receiving a State Pension when he or she died, or you are under State Pension age.

Bereavement Allowance for those under State retirement age

If you are aged at least 45 when your husband or wife dies but have not started to receive a State Retirement Pension, you should receive a Bereavement Allowance of up to £75.50 a week for 52 weeks. This is taxable. If your husband or wife had not paid sufficient National Insurance contributions, you may not get the full amount. The contribution conditions are the same as for the State Retirement Pension (explained on pages 5–8). However, if your husband or wife died as a result of an industrial accident or disease, there are no contribution conditions. Bereavement Allowance stops if you reach pension age or remarry while it is being paid.

If you are between 45 and 55 when your husband or wife dies, you may receive a reduced 'age-related' rate, which is 7 per cent lower for each year by which you are younger than 55 (so that a 45-year-old receives only 30 per cent of the full rate). These rates are decided by the age at which you start to qualify and do not change as you get older. No SERPS pension inherited from your deceased husband or wife (see below) is paid until you reach State retirement age.

If you have dependent children

If you have dependent children when your husband or wife dies, there is a Widowed Parent's Allowance whatever your age. This is £75.50, plus an addition for SERPS/S2P and plus an allowance for each child. (These will be replaced, however, by the new Child Tax Credit in 2003.)

A man who lost his wife before 9 April 2001, but who still meets the conditions, can also start claiming Widowed Parent's Allowance. However, it will not be backdated for more than three months from the date of your claim.

The Widowed Parent's Allowance is not affected by your earnings. If you remarry you will lose the Widowed Parent's Allowance. It will also be suspended during any period when you live with someone else as husband and wife. It stops when the children are no longer dependent (which means at 16, or at 19 if still in full-time education).

However, a woman who is already drawing the (now abolished) Widowed Mother's Allowance at the date of the changeover (9 April 2001) can move on to Widow's Pension under the old rules (explained below), if she is over 45 when they stop being dependent.

Reaching pension age

Once a widow reaches 60, she can draw the State Basic Pension based on her deceased husband's contributions and/or her own. A widow's entitlement will be based on her husband's contribution record if this gives a better level of pension than her own. If she is 60 or over when her husband dies and not receiving a full Basic Pension, she may be able to use his contribution record to bring her Basic Pension up to the maximum for a single person. A widower can use his wife's contribution record in the same way, *provided* that she died on or after 6 April 1979 *and* both husband and wife were over pension age when she died.

The discrimination against widowers will be ended when State retirement age is equalised from 2010.

A widow will also receive half of her husband's Graduated Pension as well as any based on her own contributions.

A widow or a widower can also draw 'Inherited' SERPS and S2P, as explained below, if they have received one of the widow's or bereavement allowances at any time during their lives, and have not remarried since.

Inherited SERPS

As SERPS was originally designed, a widow inherited the whole of her husband's SERPS pension, so long as she was eligible for the basic Widow's Pension.

In 1986 the Government made a number of changes to SERPS. One of these was that if the husband's death occurred after 5 April 2000, the widow would inherit only half his SERPS pension. This also applies to widowers, where both are over retirement age at the date of the wife's death. For reasons that no-one can explain, the DWP ignored this change in its leaflets about the subject, and in the letters officials sent to people, right up until April 1999. Many people felt they were misled and did not make additional provision when they might have done, if they had known about the change. In 2000 the Government announced some protection for those who could show they were misled.

As a result of this:

- Men and women who reach State Pension age before 5 October 2002 will be exempt from the changes. They will be able to pass on *all* of their SERPS entitlement, as now.
- The new rules will only apply in full to men and women who are 10 years or more away from State Pension age.

For anyone within 10 years of their State Pension age in October 2002, the changes will be phased in. The table below shows how this will work:

% SERPS passing to surviving spouse	Date when contributor reaches State Pension age (or would have done if they had not died earlier)
100%	3.10.2002 or earlier
90%	6.10.2002 – 5.10.2004
80%	6.10.2004 – 5.10.2006
70%	6.10.2006 – 5.10.2008
60%	6.10.2008 – 5.10.2010
50%	6.10.2010 or later

People who have evidence that they were clearly misinformed by the DWP and who are not fully covered by these proposals still have access to the usual procedures for dealing with maladministration in the Department (which can mean that an *ex gratia* payment is given).

Inherited S2P

Once this comes on stream, the widow or widower will also be able to inherit their husband's or wife's S2P. However, this will be at the 50 per cent rate from the beginning.

Benefits under the rules before April 2001

The previous rules for widow's benefits still apply for people who lost their husband or wife before 9 April 2001:

- If you had dependent children when your husband died, you may receive a Widowed Mother's Allowance, which lasts until the youngest child is 16 (or 19 if still in full-time education).
- If you did not have dependent children, but were between 55 and 64, you may receive a Widow's Pension, followed by a State Retirement Pension (see below).

- If you are aged over 55 when your Widowed Mother's Allowance runs out, you move on to the Widow's Pension at that point.
- If you are between 45 and 55 when either of these things happen, you receive a reduced 'age-related' widow's benefit.

Widowers were discriminated against under the old rules but, as explained above, those with dependent children could start drawing the new Widowed Parent's Allowance from 9 April 2001, whenever it was they lost their partner. If you are making a claim now, however, it will not be backdated more than three months.

Choosing between Widow's Pension and Retirement Pension

Widows receiving benefits under the old rules still have the choice of continuing to receive the Widow's Pension until their 65th birthday. The amounts will often be the same, but you may also receive some Graduated Pension with the Retirement Pension. Ask for a pension forecast (see page 23) six months or so before you reach 60 to check what is best.

Transitional help for older widows and widowers

People who were over 55 when the new benefits began in April 2001, and lose their husband or wife within five years, are allowed to claim means-tested Income Support without being required to follow the normal rules about seeking a job. They are also entitled to a special bereavement premium on Income Support, once the Bereavement Allowance explained above ends, to bring it up to the same rate as the Bereavement Allowance.

For further details see social security leaflet BERE *New Bereavement Benefits*.

Pension forecasts

Women under 59 years 8 months and men under 64 years 8 months can obtain a forecast of their Basic, SERPS/S2P and Graduated Pension. Fill in form BR 19 from the local social security office, and send it to the Retirement Pension Forecasting Unit in the envelope provided. (You can also obtain BR 19 on the Internet.) The forecast will tell you the amount to which you are already entitled, based on your contributions to date, and how much you will be entitled to at State Pension age, assuming you pay NI contributions until then. It explains what you might be able to do to get a better State Pension. For widowed or divorced people it tells you the amount of Basic, SERPS/S2P and Graduated Pension you are entitled to, based on your former spouse's contributions.

The forecast also allows you to check what would happen to your State Pension in different situations, such as:

- working on after pension age (page 35);
- retiring early (pages 29–34);
- going abroad (page 26);
- paying at the full rate after paying reduced-rate contributions (pages 114–117);
- paying voluntary contributions to make up for those not paid in the past (page 10); and
- getting married or divorced (pages 130–131).

Finally, it shows what difference a change in your annual earnings would make.

DRAWING YOUR PENSION

About four months before you reach pension age you should be sent a retirement pack. If you have not received one three months before your 60th/65th birthday, contact the Pension Service or your local social security office. It may be a simple slip-up, or it may mean that your age and contribution record have been wrongly recorded.

As soon as you receive this, you can:

- ring the National Tele-Claim Service and give the details over the phone;
- ring the National Tele-Claim Service and request a claim form (BR1) through the post; or
- complete and return a tear-off slip asking to be sent a form.

According to the Department of Work and Pensions (DWP), these arrangements should:

- reduce the need for it to keep going back to customers for more information, thus speeding up the rate at which claims are cleared (the DWP has found that it needs to go back to customers for more information in fewer than 2 per cent of cases, compared with 40 per cent previously); and
- reduce the need for customers to supply evidence of birth, marriage or divorce that the DWP has previously seen and verified for other purposes.

The National Tele-Claim Service is available from 7am to 7pm Monday to Friday on 0845 300 1084. Only people who have received their retirement pack should ring as it does not deal with general enquiries about pensions. The service is available for textphone users on 0845 300 2086. General enquiries should be made to the Pensions Information Line on 0845 731 3233.

Make a claim as soon as you receive the retirement pack. A married woman claiming a pension on her husband's contributions needs to make a separate claim.

If you deferred your pension when you reached 60 (women) or 65 (men) in order to gain extra pension, as explained on pages 27–28, it is your responsibility to notify your local office when you wish to start claiming your pension.

If you make a late claim for your pension, it can be backdated for up to three months. However good the reason for the delay, it will not be backdated beyond this.

Because of continuing problems with the DWP computers, it may not be possible to calculate the SERPS pension due when you retire. The DWP has given assurances that arrears will be paid and some (very limited) compensation will be given when the computer programme is finally put right.

How your pension is paid

You can choose to draw your pension in one of two ways. You can have it paid by weekly order book which you cash at a post office. Pensions are then paid one week in advance. If you cannot get to a post office someone else can cash your pension for you, as explained in the pension book.

You can also have your pension paid directly into a bank, building society or National Savings investment account by automated credit transfer. The money will then normally be paid in arrears and you can choose to receive it either four-weekly or quarterly. However, if you receive Income Support this can be paid together with your pension by automated credit transfer, weekly in advance.

Pensions of £5 a week or less (£2 or £1 per week for awards of pension prior to October 1996) are paid once a year, in December, in arrears.

Pay-day for someone retiring now is usually Monday. But if your spouse is already receiving a pension on Thursday, you can choose to have yours on the same day. You cannot receive any pension for days of retirement before your first pay-day. It is only payable for whole weeks, so it is not stopped until the end of the week in which the pensioner dies.

See social security leaflet NI 105 *Retirement Pension or Widow's Pension Paid Straight into a Bank Account*. There is also a helpline at Pension Direct on 0191 20 30 203 (Monday–Friday, 7am–7.30pm).

Going abroad or living there

If you receive your pension by weekly order book and are going abroad for less than three months, you can cash all your pension orders when you come home. However, if for some reason you have a girocheque for your pension this cannot be cashed more than a month after the date printed on it. If these rules affect you, tell your local social security office well in advance so that your pension can be paid into a bank or other account while you are away. Alternatively, arrange with them for your pension to accumulate and be paid in one lump sum on your return.

If your pension is paid into a bank or other account, you do not need to tell your local office unless you are staying abroad for more than six months. You can, if you wish, arrange to receive your pension in the country where you are staying. In most countries, the payment is made monthly, direct into a bank in that country. This tends to be the most secure method, and would generally also mean a better exchange rate than with other methods. There are special payment arrangements for pensions in India, Pakistan and Bangladesh, and for New Zealand.

If you remain abroad, the annual pension increase will be paid only in a European Union country or in one of the countries with which the UK has special arrangements (Barbados, Bermuda, Cyprus, Finland, Guernsey, Iceland, Israel, Jamaica, Jersey, Malta, Mauritius, Norway, Philippines, Sark, Sweden, Switzerland, Turkey, USA and all of former Yugoslavia). Make sure you allow yourself ample time to establish the position and make arrangements, especially if you are emigrating.

See social security leaflet GL 29 and Inland Revenue leaflet NI 38. Contact your local social security office or the Pension Service Overseas Branch (address on page 161).

INCREASING YOUR PENSION

Making voluntary contributions

If you have had an interrupted career, you may be able to increase your pension by making Class 3 voluntary contributions to cover missed years. You can do this only for gaps within the last six years. Voluntary contributions cannot be paid for years when you were paying contributions at the married woman's reduced rate (explained on pages 114–117).

Ask for a pension forecast (see page 23) before making voluntary contributions. It may be that with credits and Home Responsibilities Protection you already have a sufficient contribution record for a full pension. If, however, you have a gap which can be made up by paying one or two years' extra contributions, it may well be worthwhile.

Deferring your pension

The only other way to increase your State Basic Pension is to postpone the date when you draw it. You can choose to defer drawing your pension for a period of up to five years after State Pension age in order to earn extra pension. You cannot normally defer a pension after the age of 65 (women) or 70 (men). The period for which you defer your pension is called 'the period of enhancement'.

Once you have started drawing your pension, you can change your mind and postpone it instead, but you can only do this once. A married man whose wife is drawing a pension based on his contributions needs her consent before giving up his pension as she will have to give hers up too.

Deferring your pension increases it by about 7.5 per cent a year for each full year that you do not draw it, or by a weekly amount of ½p in the pound. You must defer it for at least seven weeks to gain any increase. Deferring your pension for the full five years increases it by about 37 per cent. Your SERPS/S2P and Graduated Pensions are increased in the same way as the Basic Pension. These rules are to change in 2010.

Deferred pension for married women

A married woman entitled to a pension on her own contributions who defers drawing it will receive an increased pension, as described above.

A married woman aged 60–64 who is entitled to a pension only on her husband's contributions can also defer this to gain an increase. If you are 60 or over and your husband is deferring his pension, you will not be able to draw the married woman's pension. Once he draws his pension, you will both receive increases.

Your pension on your husband's contributions will not be increased if, while your husband is deferring his pension, you draw a SERPS/S2P or Graduated Pension. It may be better not to draw, for example, a small amount of Graduated Pension if your husband is deferring his pension. You might receive only a few pence but you could lose pounds.

For more details see Age Concern Factsheet 19 *The State Pension.*

Is it worth deferring your pension?

Deferring a State Basic Pension is generally not worthwhile, as your heirs do not receive any advantage from it if you die before you start drawing it. Although you will pay tax on it, you might find it preferable to start drawing your pension and pay the money into a savings account. Then at least there is an asset there if anything happens to you. You could pay part or all of it into a stakeholder pension and save the Income Tax.

It is worth considering deferment, however, if drawing the State Pension would take you into a higher tax bracket (from 10 per cent to 22 per cent or from 22 per cent to 40 per cent), and you are not concerned about leaving money for others to inherit.

From 2010, the rate of increase for deferral goes up to ⅕p in the pound per week (10.4 per cent per year), and there is no limit on the length of time for which you can defer, so it will be rather more attractive.

EARLY RETIREMENT AND STATE BENEFITS

It is not possible to draw the State Pension early in the UK, as it is in some other countries. If you take early retirement from your job (whether voluntary or enforced) there are other State benefits you *may* be able to get, covering unemployment and sickness. However, the conditions for these are tight, and will become tighter still in future. If you are thinking about whether to take early retirement for whatever reason, the safest assumption is that you will receive *nothing* from the National Insurance system (and you might have to pay contributions to it) until you reach State Pension age. Base your budget on your own resources. If this means that you will find it hard to survive, you may need to think again about retiring. Means-tested Income Support will be available if you are badly off, but there is a large gap between what the State considers is enough to live on under Income Support, and what is necessary for a comfortable and enjoyable retirement.

Becoming too sick or disabled to work

People in employment will usually be covered by Statutory Sick Pay (SSP) (not dealt with in this book) for the first 28 weeks that they are too sick or disabled to work. After that, Incapacity Benefit (IB) is paid at the rate of £63.25 up to the 52nd week, and then at £70.95 for as long as you qualify. There are also age additions: £14.90 a week for people who become sick or disabled below the age of 35 and £7.45 a week for people who become sick or disabled between the ages of 35 and 45. Additions for dependent children will be paid after the 28th week. Additions for spouses are not paid at all with SSP. For IB, they are paid only where the spouse is aged 60 or over or caring for a dependent child. They are paid at a lower rate (currently £33.10 a week) for the first year, rising to £42.45 after the 52nd week.

People not entitled to SSP, for example because they are self-employed or out of work, and who become incapable of work, may get a lower rate of Incapacity Benefit (£53.50 a week) for the first 28 weeks. This is not taxable.

For all claimants, except those already on the old Invalidity Benefit when the rules changed in April 1995, the benefit is taxable.

Once you reach State Pension age (60 for women, 65 for men) you transfer over automatically to Retirement Pension.

If you retire for ill-health reasons before reaching pension age and go abroad to live, you can be denied Incapacity Benefit altogether even if you fulfil the contribution conditions. However, you do retain your right to benefit if you are moving within the European Union.

The test for Incapacity Benefit

The test of whether you are 'incapacitated', after the 28-week period, is now called the 'Personal Capability Test'. The criteria are not related to what job you could realistically find, but to your ability to perform certain functions relevant to work. These include, for example, sitting, standing, walking, lifting, manual handling, speech, comprehension, behaviour. A score is given for each of these, on a scale of severity. You receive benefits only if you score sufficiently highly on one or several of these.

In a few pilot regions there is at present also an assessment by the Medical Services doctor about what work you *are* capable of doing. This will be sent to the adviser in your local social security office (called 'Jobcentre Plus' under the DWP's reorganisation) who is dealing with you.

Some groups do not have to undergo the medical test:

- people who receive the highest rate of the care component of Disability Living Allowance; and
- people with certain chronic or severe conditions (a detailed list of these is included in social security leaflet IB 214).

People who were receiving Invalidity Benefit on 13 April 1995 when the scheme changed, but do not come into one of the protected groups, are also subject to the incapacity test.

However, for as long as they retain their benefit (without a break of eight weeks or more), it is not taxable, and their benefit rate is protected and uprated in further years. Their SERPS pension, which was paid with Invalidity Benefit but is not paid with Incapacity Benefit for new claimants, is frozen at the April 1994 level. They can also receive uprated Invalidity Allowance, based on their age when they first got sick, but this is offset against any SERPS pension they get.

You may be told that you are not sick enough to qualify for Incapacity Benefit although you or your employer consider that you are too sick for work. Ask for advice from a Citizens Advice Bureau or other advice agency. Many people who are turned down for Incapacity Benefit appeal to an independent Social Security Appeal Tribunal, and find that they are then granted the benefit.

National Insurance contribution requirements

As well as the medical tests, there are rules about the number of National Insurance contributions you must have paid:

- at some point in your working life, you must have actually *paid* contributions, on earnings of at least 25 times the Lower Earnings Limit (explained on page 8) for that year, in one tax year out of the last three years in the calendar year before you make your claim (but see page 9 if your earnings are between the LEL and the Earnings Threshold); and
- within the last two tax years before the calendar year in which you make your claim, you must have either paid or been credited with contributions on earnings of at least 50 times the Lower Earnings Limit in those years.

The main effect of this (and the idea behind it) is that if you have been unemployed or early retired for a time before you fall ill, you may not be able to claim Incapacity Benefit whatever the medical test says.

Occupational and personal pensions and Incapacity Benefit

If you have been on Incapacity Benefit since before April 2001, and you continue to qualify, it will be paid in full no matter what your other income. For new IB claims after that date, however, if you have more than £85 a week of occupational pension, personal pension, or Permanent Health Insurance (PHI) payment provided by your employer, your IB will be reduced by 50p for every £1 of your pension income above this limit. However, you avoid this deduction if the PHI is paid through your employer's payroll (as it usually is).

Example

Adriana has had to take early retirement due to stress and has an occupational pension of £115 a week. To find out what IB she will lose:

deduct £85, leaving £30
divide £30 by 2 = £15
So she will lose £15 of her IB.

Once someone who was claiming under the pre-April 2001 rules has a break in their entitlement of eight weeks or more, they lose the proection of those rules and come under the same framework as anyone else.

See social security leaflet SD3 *Long Term Ill or Disabled*. Age Concern Books annual publication *Your Rights* gives information about all State benefits.

Jobseeker's Allowance

If you have taken early retirement but do not qualify for IB, you may be able to claim contribution-based Jobseeker's Allowance (JSA) for up to 26 weeks provided that you have paid sufficient NI contributions. To qualify you must be unemployed and actively seeking work.

You may be disqualified from JSA for up to 26 weeks if you leave a job voluntarily 'without just cause'. If you have chosen to accept early retirement, you may therefore be disqualified from benefit. If this happens, seek advice from a Citizens Advice Bureau or other advice agency.

Jobseeker's Allowance comes in two forms; contribution-based and income-based. Contribution-based JSA is paid for up to six months, if you qualify because you have made the right National Insurance contributions. However, it is only paid for you as an individual, not for your spouse or family, and it is only £53.95 a week (for those aged 25 or over) in 2002–2003. Income-based JSA is intended to provide money for them from the start, and for you once the six months are up. As the name suggests, it is means-tested – ie, both your income and your capital are taken into account in deciding whether you qualify.

If you receive an occupational or personal pension, contribution-based JSA will be reduced by the amount your pension exceeds £50.

If you have capital of more than £8,000 (£12,000 if you are aged 60 or over), you will not be entitled to claim income-based JSA (even if your weekly income is low), so then you will receive contribution-based JSA for six months only and no State benefits thereafter.

If your spouse or partner works 24 hours a week or more, there will be no entitlement for either of you to income-based JSA (although you might be eligible for Family Credit).

You also have to show that you are 'actively seeking work'. All claimants have to sign a Jobseeker's Agreement, committing them to take certain steps to find a job.

Redundancy pay

There are statutory minimum figures for redundancy payments, but you may find your employer offers a better package. Some elements of these payments, such as money in lieu of notice, can prevent you receiving JSA for the weeks they are expected to cover. Get advice from the Citizens Advice Bureau or your trade union if you have been affected in this way or if you feel your redundancy pay has been wrongly calculated.

Where an employee is within 12 months of his or her 65th birthday, the statutory redundancy entitlement is reduced by one-twelfth for each complete month after the 64th birthday. This 'tapering' gradually reduces entitlement to nothing by the time the employee reaches the age of 65.

If you are within 90 weeks of the retirement age set by your employer, it is legally allowable for redundancy pay to be reduced or even lost altogether by 'offsetting' it against the value of the pension rights. Good employers rarely do this, however, except perhaps as part of a more generous early retirement package. Older employees who suspect that they may be made redundant should check in advance whether this offsetting will apply. You must be notified if this is to be applied to you.

See Department of Trade and Industry leaflet PL 808 (available from Jobcentres, Citizens Advice Bureaux and libraries).

Protecting your State Pension in early retirement

If you are planning to retire early, check whether you have paid enough NI contributions to receive a full Basic Pension when you reach pension age. You can do this by getting a pension forecast: contact your local social security office and ask for form BR 19, as explained on page 23.

You will receive NI credits towards your pension if you are drawing a benefit such as Jobseeker's Allowance or Incapacity Benefit. If you are under 60 and seeking work, it could well be worth registering for Jobseeker's Allowance – even if you are not entitled to benefit – in order to receive credits. If you are a man aged 60–64, you will automatically receive credits even though you are not signing on as unemployed or receiving another benefit, as long as you are not self-employed or abroad for more than half the year.

If you are not entitled to credits and have an incomplete NI record, you may want to consider paying Class 3 voluntary contributions (see page 10).

WORKING AFTER PENSION AGE

Once you have reached State Pension age (60 for women, 65 for men), and provided you satisfy the contribution conditions, you can draw your State Pension. If you decide to carry on working or to take another job, your State Pension will not be affected by the amount you earn or the number of hours you work.

Check whether your earnings will affect any means-tested benefits you might be entitled to, or you could find that you lose more than you gain by working.

You will be liable to pay Income Tax on your pension and your earnings (your tax code will be adjusted to take into account any pension you receive), but you will not have to pay NI contributions. You should receive a certificate of exemption from the DWP to give to your employer. Your employer will still have to pay its share of NI contributions for you.

As explained on pages 27–28, you can choose to defer drawing your pension for a period of up to five years after pension age in order to earn extra pension, although this may not be worthwhile.

● **If your pension is small and you do not have much in the way of savings, you may be entitled to Income Support (also known as Minimum Income Guarantee) from the DWP and/or Housing Benefit and Council Tax Benefit from the local authority. These are means-tested benefits, which means that they are payable only to people whose income and capital are below a certain level. These benefits are not covered in this book. See Age Concern Books annual publication *Your Rights* for full details.**

Occupational Pensions

Between 10 and 11 million employees – just under half the working population – are currently active members of occupational pension schemes (also called 'company' pension schemes or, in the public sector, 'superannuation'). Around six million people receive payments from such schemes. Over half the people who have retired in recent years have had some sort of occupational pension.

This chapter looks at the different types of occupational pension scheme, earnings-related or money-purchase, contracted in or out of SERPS; drawing your pension; and how to increase your pension by paying extra contributions or carrying on working after retirement age. It also discusses what happens to your pension if you change job or retire early.

ARE YOU IN AN OCCUPATIONAL PENSION SCHEME?

Many employers, especially the larger ones, offer a pension arrangement to their employees as part of their package of non-wage benefits. There are two main ways of doing this:

- through an occupational pension scheme (also called a 'company scheme' or 'superannuation'); or
- through a Group Personal Pension (GPP) or stakeholder pension.

It is not always easy to tell the difference between them from the literature that employers put out. It is important, however, because the law, and the limits on what can be paid in and drawn as pension, are different. You should be able to find out what sort of scheme yours is by looking at the scheme booklet. If it explains that the scheme has *trustees* looking after it, it is almost certainly an occupational scheme. (There are a very few personal/stakeholder schemes which also have trustees, including the one run by the TUC.) In local government and some other public sector employment, there are *statutory* schemes, which do not have trustees but have Acts of Parliament covering them instead; these are also occupational.

If you cannot establish what sort of scheme it is from the booklet, there should be a contact name and phone number there for you to ask.

The tasks of trustees, and who they will be, are covered on pages 138–139. GPPs and stakeholder pensions are covered in the next chapter.

HOW OCCUPATIONAL PENSION SCHEMES WORK

There are two main types of occupational scheme. The first is an earnings-related (also called defined benefit) scheme. In this, you are promised a pension as a proportion of your earnings, and the percentage of pay that goes in as contributions may vary over time, to ensure that the promise is met. The other sort is a money-purchase (defined contribution) scheme, where the percentage contribution is fixed but the pension depends on the investment results. (There are also 'hybrid' schemes which include elements of both.) These two different types are explained in more detail in the sections below.

Usually, both employer and employees contribute to the pension scheme, but some schemes are 'non-contributory'. This means that the employer alone contributes. They are more common in the financial services industry than elsewhere, and among senior executives.

Earnings-related schemes

These are the traditional type of pension schemes, and if you have worked for a larger employer for a while you probably have one of these. As they are generally linked to your earnings close to retirement, they are often called 'final salary' or 'final earnings' schemes.

With an earnings-related (or defined benefit) scheme, you (or your employer alone) pay contributions into a pension fund. The benefits are calculated by reference to the length of time you have been a member of the scheme and your 'final pensionable earnings' (which might also be called 'salary', 'pay' or 'remuneration', in your scheme). Your 'final pensionable earnings' are multiplied by an 'accrual rate' and then multiplied by the years and part-years for which you have been a scheme member.

The 'accrual rate' is the fraction of your final pensionable earnings you receive for every year of scheme membership, usually $\frac{1}{60}$ or $\frac{1}{80}$ (sometimes expressed as a percentage). With an accrual rate of $\frac{1}{80}$ you will normally have to belong to a scheme for 40 years to get a pension of half these earnings ($\frac{40}{80}$). If the accrual rate is $\frac{1}{60}$, 40 years in the scheme will entitle you to $\frac{40}{60}$ of your earnings at retirement, that is, two-thirds of your earnings. Some schemes have different accrual rates for different ages, or allow you to choose different rates (and contribution levels).

Your 'final pensionable earnings' may be an average of your earnings over the last two or three years, or years further back if your earnings have dropped as you come up to retirement. Some schemes provide a pension based on earnings in the last 12 months, or the last tax year. Sometimes only part of your pay is pensionable. Schemes may be 'integrated' or have 'clawback' with the State Basic Pension – meaning that they deduct an amount from your pay linked to the State Pension, before calculating the pension. Alternatively, the scheme's pension may be calculated on the basis of your full pay, but then have all, or a proportion of, the State Basic Pension deducted from it.

The argument is that the State is pensioning that element, so the scheme need not do so. Not surprisingly, this is very unpopular with members and there are a number of campaigns against it. Features like this can make a sizeable difference to the amount you get, so check the scheme booklet.

Integrating the employer's pension with the State scheme bears especially hard on the lower paid, and it can also mean that people are deceived into thinking that the scheme is better than it is. A scheme that gives $\frac{1}{80}$ of all earnings can be better for the lower paid than one that gives $\frac{1}{60}$ of earnings on an integrated basis.

In most cases, either you can choose to turn part of your pension into a tax-free lump sum at retirement, or the lump sum comes automatically attached to the pension. The amount you can take as a lump sum, and the advantages and disadvantages of taking the maximum you are allowed, are discussed on pages 53–54.

Money-purchase schemes

The other type of scheme, the money-purchase scheme, works in very much the same way as any other private investment. The contributions that the scheme member and the employer are making and the investment returns on them, go into an individual 'pot' which is then used for the pension. Often, the employer matches the contributions that the employee is making, although there are cases where employees are paying much the larger share, and others where the employer is making the whole contribution.

There will often be a choice of different investment funds into which to put your contributions, some less risky than others. Many schemes offer also a 'default' option, where your money is put if you do not make a choice yourself. This may be what is called a 'lifestyle' fund, which means that it is invested to start with in company shares (which can be risky but tend to do better in the long run) and is then moved into safer but lower-return investments such as gilts (lending money to the Government) as you come up to retirement.

At retirement, part of the 'pot' is paid out in a tax-free lump sum, and the rest goes to buy an annuity (see page 95). Many schemes provide an 'open market option' which means that the scheme administrator shops around for the best annuity rate available at the time. It is possible in some schemes to defer buying the annuity and draw money direct from your fund. These features are very similar to those in personal pensions, so they are considered in more detail in that chapter.

Money-purchase schemes have been around for a very long time, but their numbers have grown in recent years. In particular, a number of very large employers have said recently that no new starters may join their final-earnings scheme, but must go into the money-purchase one instead (the section below offers some reasons for this).

How the different types compare

The advantage for employers of money-purchase schemes is that they know the costs. Money is paid into an investment fund in respect of each employee, and whatever is in that fund – be it a lot or very little – is used to buy the employee's pension at whatever the annuity rates are at the time of retirement. The disadvantage for employees is that they do not know what pension they will get, as they depend on future interest rates, the charges made and the investment performance of the fund.

The opposite is true with earnings-related schemes. As an employee you know what proportion of your final earnings you are likely to receive as a pension, depending on the accrual rate and how long you have been a member of the scheme. Although you cannot be sure what your final earnings will be, you do know to what extent your standard of living will be protected when you retire.

It is different from the employer's point of view. An employee's earnings at retirement date can only be estimated in advance, and hence also the cost of building up a pension for that person. As explained on pages 143–144, this has worked to the advantage of employers in recent years, because schemes have built up substantial surplus funds. But the reverse is now beginning to happen, with schemes building up deficits.

Earnings-related schemes do, however, have disadvantages for those who move jobs frequently, as 'early leavers' tend to be penalised. This is because your pension for those years is then based on your earnings when you left that job rather than your final earnings at retirement. This pension is not frozen, but it is increased at best in line with prices, while earnings would be expected to go up rather faster. So although in general earnings-related schemes have the edge, they may not be the best option for highly mobile workers, or people on short-term contracts, or people who will have gaps in their employment.

For most people it is wise to join an earnings-related scheme or a good money-purchase one if your employer offers you one. Your options if you then leave the job are discussed on pages 62–71.

Inland Revenue limits

There are top limits laid down by the Inland Revenue on the amount you can receive as an occupational pension from a tax-approved scheme (a scheme under which you receive tax relief on pension contributions). The major restriction is that you cannot receive more than two-thirds of your final 'remuneration' as a pension (but see page 84 for details of who is able to buy extra pension above this limit with a 'concurrent' stakeholder policy).

There is also a ceiling of £97,200 (in 2002–2003) on the annual earnings that can be taken into account (called the 'earnings cap'). Those who have earnings above this level can still receive a pension based on them, but the scheme must be 'unapproved', which means it does not receive the same tax relief. The ceiling does not affect those who were already members of their current scheme before 1 June 1989.

Finally, there is a ceiling on contributions. Employees can contribute up to 15 per cent of their earnings to an occupational scheme, including any Additional Voluntary Contributions (see pages 56–61). There is no percentage limit on the employer's contribution (except for some top executives' schemes), but they are not allowed to put in 'excessive' amounts. In practice, the average employer's contribution is currently about 9 per cent of earnings, or 11 per cent if the scheme is non-contributory for the member (according to the National Association of Pension Funds 2001 survey).

● **If you are in an occupational scheme and you earn less than £30,000 a year, you may be able to put up to £3,600 a year into a stakeholder pension on top of these limits (see page 84 for details).**

Money-purchase schemes – opting in to new tax rules

Since April 2001 there have been new tax rules for some pension schemes. These new rules mainly affect stakeholder and personal pension schemes, but it will be possible for occupational money-purchase schemes to opt into the new system as well. The details of these new rules are explained in the next chapter on pages 83–84. Very few schemes are opting to change. Any that do will have to inform the members, probably in advance, as they will have to change a number of their rules.

If your scheme does opt to change, you will then be allowed to pay into a combination of different pensions (occupational, personal, stakeholder) at the same time, so long as you do not go above the Inland Revenue limits overall. These limits will also only be on the contributions that you can pay in, and not on the amount of pension you can draw out. However, you will have to put in a considerable amount, or be very lucky with your investments, to achieve anything close to the current benefit limits.

Contracted in or out of S2P?

The employer, and in some cases also the employees, choose whether the pension scheme is 'contracted in' or 'contracted out' of S2P (explained on pages 14–16). If it is contracted in, their employees receive S2P as well as the occupational pension. The Inland Revenue treats the S2P pension as quite separate, so you are then allowed to receive the maximum occupational pension of two-thirds of your final pay as well.

If an employer's scheme meets certain requirements, it can be contracted out and replace S2P in part or in full. (How S2P works was explained on pages 12–14). In contracted-out occupational schemes, both employers and employees pay lower NI contributions. This reduction or rebate represents the cost of the S2P benefit which is lost through contracting out.

- Individuals can also contract out of S2P by taking out an 'appropriate personal pension', as explained on pages 76–78, if they belong to a contracted-in occupational scheme or no scheme at all.

What a contracted-out scheme must provide

To be allowed to contract out of S2P (and previously SERPS), the scheme must meet some minimum standards, but these have changed over time.

Pension built up before 1997

In a contracted-out salary-related scheme (called a COSR in the jargon) up until April 1997 the law said that the occupational pension built up must not be less than a Guaranteed Minimum Pension (GMP) which is roughly the same as you would have had if you had remained in SERPS. This had to override the normal scheme rules.

Example

Tony's pension scheme was contracted out, and the normal scheme rules said that only basic pay was pensionable. But Tony did a lot of shiftwork, and under the rules the Guaranteed Minimum Pension (GMP) was calculated taking account of this as well. So when Tony came up to retirement, the scheme administrator did two sets of calculations, on the normal rules and the GMP rules. Since the GMP was higher, this was what Tony received.

COSR schemes also have to pay a widow's and a widower's GMPs, but there is not full equality here. Widows' GMPs have existed since the system started in 1978, and so they are half the member's GMP built up since 1978. Widowers' GMPs, however, only began in 1988, so they are only half the member's GMP built up since 1988. In both cases, the widow's or widower's GMP need only be paid if the spouse is aged over 45, or has dependent children. (In practice, many schemes are rather more generous and pay them at any age.)

Changes in April 1997

These rules changed in 1997, when the guarantee that no-one could lose by being contracted out through a COSR scheme disappeared for future service (GMPs built up in the past are protected). Instead, the scheme must be certified to be of the same standard as or better than a 'reference scheme' for at least 90 per cent of the membership. The idea is that most people will not lose out on pension compared to the position in SERPS.

Employers' schemes now have to provide inflation-proofing on pensions – both in payment and while they are deferred – on their own instead of sharing responsibility with the State. The maximum requirement for increases is now limited to 5 per cent a year. This means that the risks of high levels of inflation are carried by the employees and pensioners, and people in contracted-out schemes will carry the risk of ending up with worse benefits than if they had remained in SERPS/S2P.

Protected Rights

Most money-purchase schemes are contracted in to SERPS/S2P. Some, however, are contracted out. These generally come under the rules for contracted-out money-purchase schemes (COMPs). In these, the minimum requirement is about the money that goes in, rather than the pension which emerges at the other end. At the minimum, the National Insurance rebate (explained on pages 48–49) must be invested to create a Protected Rights fund for each individual. When you retire, this can only be used to buy a particular type of annuity – one that increases by 3 per cent for service before 6 April 1997, and 5 per cent (or the rise in the Retail Prices Index if that is lower) for service after that date. The annuity rate used to work out how much pension your pot of money can buy must also be equal for men and women. The Protected Rights fund cannot be paid out as a lump sum.

When your SERPS/S2P pension entitlement is being calculated, you are assumed to be getting as much from your COMP as you would have had from SERPS/S2P for those years, so a deduction is made from the State benefit.

If a member dies in service leaving a widow or widower, the accumulated fund is used to buy a survivor's annuity (and to provide a lump sum if more than the minimum has been going into the scheme).

To confuse matters further, some final earnings schemes are contracted out by this Protected Rights route (because an employer can save money that way) and therefore follow other rules, rather than those explained above. You will get the normal pension promise under the final salary rule but this cannot be less than the pension that could be bought by your Protected Rights investments.

Deciding whether to contract out of S2P

In a contracted-out salary-related (COSR) scheme, the decision about whether to contract out is taken by the employer, and is reviewed every three years. However in a money-purchase scheme, the decision as to whether or not it is sensible to contract out of S2P is normally yours.

It depends largely on your age. This is because one of the most important influences on the amount of pension you receive from a money-purchase scheme is your age when each contribution goes in. The younger you are, the more time your money has to build up interest or dividends, and so the more there will be when you retire. Or, to put it the other way round, when you are older, you have to put in much more money to achieve the same pension. The level of your earnings is also important. So most (although not all) of these schemes are set up with two sections; one contracted out and one contracted in. The member then chooses which one to belong to.

Example

Bill and **Mary** both start paying into a money-purchase scheme at the same time. Bill is 20 and Mary is 40. Their pension scheme achieves an average annual rate of return of 7 per cent. The table below shows how their original investment grows over the decades, up to the time they reach 60 and retire.

(The 7 per cent figure is taken for the sake of this illustration, because it so happens that with compound interest at 7 per cent an investment doubles in money value over ten years; the gap between Bill and Mary would be much larger if the interest rate was higher.)

Age	Bill £	Mary £
20	1,000	
30	2,000	
40	4,000	1,000
50	8,000	2,000
60	16,000	4,000

If Mary wants the same amount of pension from her contribution at 40 as Bill will have from his at 20, she must put in several times as much money. For Bill, the rebate for contracting out of S2P may well be enough to give him a pension better than the State; for Mary it is less likely to be.

● **This age factor applies with a personal pension too, and is considered further on pages 77–78. It does not apply with earnings-related pensions, where the accrual rate is almost always the same at all ages.**

The rebate for contracting out of SERPS/S2P via a money-purchase occupational pension (a COMP) is age-related. This means that the older you are (up to the age of 50), the more money is paid from the National Insurance Fund into the scheme for your pension.

This works in a complicated way; each time the employer pays you, it will pay the full rebate from *your* NI contributions (1.6 per cent of your earnings between the lower and upper limits) into the pension scheme. But it will pay a rebate of only 1 per cent from *its* NI contributions into the scheme. The DWP will then check your age and pay over the rest of what is due (up to an additional 7.9 per cent for someone aged 52 or over) later in the year.

This system relies heavily on the DWP records of ages, and the computer system, being right. It is worth checking your payslips, and any information you receive from the pension scheme or the DWP, and querying it if it seems wrong.

As you get older, or if your wages drop, it may not be worth continuing to contract out of SERPS/S2P. Anyone in their 40s or 50s should check with the pension administrator.

For more information see the *FSA Guide to Contracting Out of SERPS* or the DWP guide PM 7 *Contracted-out Pensions: Your guide*.

Protection for dependants

Lump-sum benefit

Generally, there is a lump-sum 'death benefit' or 'life-assurance benefit' if a member of an occupational scheme (of either sort) dies at any time while working for that employer. Sometimes this benefit (perhaps at a lower level) also covers people who are too young, or have not worked for the employer for long enough, to join the scheme yet.

The Inland Revenue allows schemes to pay a maximum death benefit of four times the member's earnings, plus a refund of the member's contributions with interest. This lump sum is usually paid to a 'beneficiary' nominated by the member or selected by the trustees.

There is usually a nomination form in the scheme booklet, or available from the pensions administrator. It could also be called an 'expression of wish form' or a 'letter of wishes'. These names make clear one important point – it is the trustees, not the member, who have the final decision on where the money should go. This is for two reasons: firstly, it means that the money is not technically the property of the member at the point of death, so it is not caught for Inheritance Tax. Secondly, it allows the trustees to take the real circumstances into account, if perhaps someone has not changed their nomination for many years or has asked for something that seems unreasonable. The trustees have a duty to act as 'reasonable and prudent people, not frivolously or maliciously', but, nonetheless, many people do resent their involvement in this.

If you want to be as sure as you can that they will follow your wishes:

- keep your nomination form up to date, and review it whenever your circumstances change; and
- if you are asking the trustees to do something which they might think unusual, add a letter explaining the reasons.

Example

Laurence is a widower, with two sons who are doing very well for themselves and one who has never been able to hold down a job, as he has bouts of very bad depression. Laurence has agreed with the two other sons that they will always look after the third, and so he wants the pension scheme's death benefit to go to them jointly, to be held in trust for the third. He puts the bare facts on his nomination form, and adds a letter signed by all his sons, spelling out what they have agreed.

In some public sector pension schemes, however, the lump sum is treated as part of your estate, so you can leave it in your will.

Once an employee reaches retirement age, this life assurance benefit usually disappears, although there are a few schemes which offer a flat-rate 'funeral benefit'. The Inland Revenue rules say that the maximum payable is £2,500.

Five-year guarantee

Most schemes have a five-year guarantee. This means that if a member dies in the first five years of retirement, the unpaid balance of five years' pension can be given as a lump sum, or possibly a continuing pension. A lump sum may be the full balance of the five years' money or it may be 'discounted'. This means that the amount may be reduced to take account of the interest the fund could have earned on the money over the years if it had not been paid out all at once.

Pensions for dependants

If a scheme member dies in service, there is usually a pension for a widow or widower. The Inland Revenue allows this to be a maximum of two-thirds of the member's projected pension based on service to the normal retirement date. When pensions for children are added, the total must not exceed the member's maximum projected pension. However, most earnings-related schemes give a half pension rather than two-thirds, and many money-purchase schemes give only a pension bought out of the fund that has built up for the member by the time they die. This could be very small if the member is young.

When the death takes place after retirement, there is usually also a widow or widower's pension. This can be two-thirds of the member's own but is more often half. However, it is usually based on the full pension entitlement before any reduction because a lump sum has been taken – and as uprated once in payment.

Check that the death benefits offered by your own scheme are adequate. If not, raise the matter with the scheme trustees.

● **If you and your partner are not married, check whether the spouse's pension can be paid to a 'financial dependant'. Many schemes do not allow for this. This will make it even more important to complete, and keep up to date, a nomination form for the death benefit, so that at least the lump sum can be paid to your partner.**

See pages 131–133 for details about what happens about occupational pensions when a couple divorce.

If you run a business

For small businesses, the small self-administered scheme (SSAS) is an option worth considering, as it allows you to make larger pension contributions while still using the money in your business.

'Self-investment' – investing in the employing company's shares, loans to the company, or property occupied by it – of more than 5 per cent of the fund is not generally allowed in occupational pension schemes. In an SSAS, however, a far higher proportion of the fund can be used to buy assets for the business, such as an office or building from which it is run. The business then pays rent to the fund.

An SSAS can have no more than 11 members in all, and if the 'self-investment' option is used, then all members must be trustees, and all trustees' decisions must be unanimous. There must also be an outside 'pensioneer' trustee (an expert who is there to see that the Inland Revenue's special rules for these schemes are kept).

Anyone contemplating this sort of arrangement should obtain specialist advice from an actuarial firm. Setting-up costs are high, and unlikely to be worthwhile unless the total annual contribution will be at least £20,000.

DRAWING YOUR PENSION

Almost every pension scheme in the private sector allows you to turn part of your pension into a lump sum on retirement, and this is tax-free. This is called 'commuting' the pension. Typically, a man of 65 has to give up £1,000 a year of pension to receive a lump sum of £9,000. If you are younger, or a woman, you will have to give up less to receive the same amount.

There are Inland Revenue restrictions on the amount you can have as a lump sum. You can normally take ³⁄₈₀ of your final earnings for each year of service up to a maximum of 40 years. Alternatively, your scheme can allow you to take a lump sum that is two and a quarter times your annual pension worked out before commutation. Some schemes allow anyone with service of 20 years or more to take the maximum amount – check your own scheme rules. However, your Guaranteed Minimum Pension (or Protected Rights Pension in a contracted-out money-purchase (COMP) scheme) has to be taken as a pension, and cannot be commuted to a lump sum. There are also limits on commuting pension you build up from Additional Voluntary Contributions (AVCs), as explained on page 57.

Most people like to take the largest possible tax-free lump sum rather than taking the whole amount as taxable pension income, both because of the tax advantage and because it gives you more options. However, if your scheme gives good pension increases or has a guarantee of index-linking, it could make sense to take the pension and let the cash go. The rate at which you exchange the pension for cash can also vary considerably. In a scheme with a poor commutation rate it may not be worthwhile.

In some public service schemes, such as those in the Civil Service and the NHS, it is almost automatic that you receive both a pension (smaller than a good private sector pension) and a lump sum. There are some exceptions in cases where you join the scheme as a late entrant. There is therefore generally no need to 'commute' any of your pension. In theory, the scheme rules often allow you to turn part of your lump sum back into pension, but the lure of the tax-free money is such that it is hardly ever done.

See pages 72–74 for the position if you want to draw your pension early, or page 61 if you decide to go on working after pension age.

Income drawdown from an occupational scheme

If you belong to a money-purchase scheme, it may be possible to defer buying an annuity when you retire, and instead to draw income direct from the fund for some years. Alternatively, you may be able to transfer your fund to a personal pension in order to do the same thing.

Living off the fund in this way is called 'income drawdown', and is quite popular among those with larger pension funds. It carries quite a lot of risks, however, and the Government has imposed some strict regulations about it. The details of income drawdown are covered on pages 103–105, under personal pensions.

● It is essential that you receive good financial advice before taking any decisions on income drawdown from a money-purchase scheme. See the FSA's *Guide to Financial Advice* for information on how to obtain this.

INCREASING YOUR PENSION

Employees aiming for a pension worth two-thirds of their final pensionable earnings need to spend 40 years in a pension scheme that gives $\frac{1}{60}$ of salary for each year of service. If you have had a varied or broken career pattern, your pension benefits could be far smaller. If your pension is based on $\frac{1}{80}$ of final earnings, then 40 years will give you only half pay. The calculation of the pension may in any case be based on less than total earnings. You may therefore want to think about making extra contributions to your pension scheme, or about paying into another (stakeholder) scheme in addition.

The maximum permitted contribution by an employee to the employer's scheme is 15 per cent of earnings. Most employees pay only around 5 or 6 per cent. So there is room to increase your contributions to your employer's pension scheme by taking out Additional Voluntary Contributions (AVCs and FSAVCs), as described below.

Sometimes a senior employee can arrange a 'salary sacrifice' in return for higher pension contributions from the employer. This has to follow certain rules to be tax-efficient and should be discussed with your own and the company accountant. If you have earnings above the pensions 'cap' (currently £97,200 a year in 2002–2003 for those who have moved jobs since 1989), then extra pension taking account of these earnings must come from an 'unapproved' scheme which does not have the same tax advantages.

The older you are, the less time you have to contribute to a pension fund and for your contribution to grow in value. So if you are paying the extra over only a short period, you will need to put in the maximum the Inland Revenue allows. This may not be as unrealistic as it sounds, since an older person may well have fewer financial commitments. At the same time the need for an adequate retirement income becomes more apparent.

Your pension may also be increased if you delay drawing it because you decide to work beyond retirement age, as explained on page 61.

Additional Voluntary Contributions

Additional Voluntary Contributions (AVCs) can be paid by anyone who is already a member of an employer's pension scheme, and all schemes must have an arrangement for them.

AVCs allow you to increase your benefits, provided you do not exceed the Inland Revenue's limits. They are also useful if part of your pay – for instance shift premiums or overtime pay – is not counted as pensionable within the employer's scheme.

Details of the scheme operated by your employer can be obtained from your pensions administrator, trade union representative or personnel officer. They may be included in the scheme booklet or there may be a separate leaflet. Some schemes operate their own arrangements, but most buy in this facility from one of the major insurance companies or building societies. In some cases, when you start drawing the pension from the main scheme, your AVCs are used to buy you an extra annuity (explained on pages 95–102) within the scheme. This usually gives you a more favourable rate than if you buy the annuity from the insurance company or on the open market, which are the other alternatives.

If you are in a public service scheme, you can use your AVCs to buy 'added years', thus increasing your main pension. A few private sector schemes allow this, but in most private schemes AVCs are available only on a money-purchase basis (explained on page 41).

Inland Revenue limits

The Inland Revenue puts two major restrictions on AVCs. The first is that the maximum contribution by an employee into an AVC and employer's pension scheme combined may not exceed 15 per cent of an employee's total earnings. There is full tax relief on these contributions, given through the PAYE system as with main scheme contributions.

The second restriction is that total benefits from an AVC and main pension scheme combined must not exceed the Inland

Revenue's limits, as explained on page 43. The main restriction is that the pension must not be more than two-thirds of total earnings at retirement. If your pension reaches the maximum allowed, you are entitled to rearrange the benefits so that all the other elements, such as the annual increases and the spouse's pension, also come up to the Inland Revenue limits.

Taking a refund

If you exceed the limits, the Inland Revenue insists that the fund returns any excess AVCs plus the investment returns, and this is then taxed. The rates are 32 per cent for basic-rate taxpayers and just under 46 per cent for those paying the higher rate.

These figures are intended to take account of the fact that you received tax relief originally both on the payments into the pension fund and on the investment income, and to put you in the same position as if you had used another savings vehicle. So you will not lose directly if you have to take a refund, but you will have lost the use of your money in earlier years when you might have wanted to spend it. There is no point, therefore, in deliberately putting too much into AVCs, nor should the scheme administrator allow this.

Taking a lump sum from AVCs

The Inland Revenue rules are that unless you were already paying AVCs before April 1987, the AVC fund must be used to provide a pension and none of it be commuted into a lump sum. This may mean that you cannot take the maximum tax-free lump sum that the Inland Revenue would otherwise allow. However, for many people it is still possible to take as much as you are allowed to have from the main scheme pension, and then replace it with the AVC pension.

Other restrictions on AVCs

Some schemes put their own restrictions on how and when you can pay into AVCs, as they are allowed to do under Inland

Revenue rules. The scheme may refuse to accept contributions below 0.5 per cent of either your taxable earnings or three times the Lower Earnings Limit (currently £75 a week), whichever is the higher, in any tax year. Otherwise, you can vary the amounts and timing of your AVCs as much as the scheme allows – but any limits set by the scheme should not be 'unreasonable'. Schemes often allow you to put in an extra lump sum, perhaps from an annual bonus, so long as you remain within the Inland Revenue limits. If necessary, you could make two payments, one in March and one in April (and so in different tax years), to keep within the 15 per cent limit.

Free Standing Additional Voluntary Contributions

Free Standing Additional Voluntary Contributions (FSAVCs) have the same aim as AVCs: to increase retirement benefits. The major difference is that FSAVCs are sold by independent providers – insurance companies, building societies and others – rather than being set up and administered within the company. This means that the charges are likely to be considerably higher.

Basic-rate and higher-rate taxpayers get tax relief on FSAVC contributions, but in a different way from AVCs. With FSAVCs, employees pay contributions net of the basic rate, which is then claimed by the pension provider from the Inland Revenue. Higher-rate taxpayers then claim higher-rate relief via the annual tax return.

Inland Revenue limits

There is a 'headroom check' to ensure that the benefits from the main company scheme and an FSAVC taken together do not exceed Inland Revenue limits. This is a calculation done by the FSAVC provider with the co-operation of the main scheme administrator. It need be done only when FSAVC premiums exceed £200 a month or £2,400 a year. The Inland Revenue limits are the same for AVCs or FSAVCs, so there is no point in trying to overfund through separate FSAVC payments.

Stakeholder/personal pensions

As explained in more detail on pages 84–85, since April 2001 the large majority of people in occupational schemes have *also* been able to pay in up to £3,600 a year into a stakeholder (or other personal) pension. If you can afford to do this as well as pay AVCs, you will end up with a higher pension as a result, and can even go above the normal two-thirds limit explained above. Most people, however, will have to treat stakeholder pensions as an alternative to AVCs as a method of increasing their pension.

AVCs, FSAVCs or stakeholder pensions?

The in-house AVC is generally likely to be better value than an FSAVC. In many cases, the employer pays the charges which are made by the insurance company or other provider, or has been able to negotiate a low rate. AVC charges have in any case come down recently, because of competition from stakeholder pensions. There are, however, some poor quality AVC arrangements around, where the charges and penalties are as steep as if you were buying the policy individually. There are also some where the investment choice is very poor. The scheme trustees should be able to negotiate better terms, and should be pressed on this if they have not done so.

FSAVC charges have also dropped, but may still be quite high and you could find you are paying commission to those who have sold the policy to you. A rule of thumb is that you could lose around 20 per cent of your contributions, in commission payments and administration, with the average FSAVC. In many, the bulk of these costs will come at the beginning of your policy ('front end loaded', in the jargon). If you are thinking of taking out an FSAVC to increase your investment choice, consider whether the returns will be so much better that they outweigh these extra costs.

The Financial Services Authority (FSA) requires anyone selling you an FSAVC to point out the in-house AVC options, and to say that, in most circumstances, this would be a better buy.

Some people have been wrongly advised to take out FSAVCs when they would have been better off staying with their in-house scheme. The FSA has ordered insurance companies and financial advisers to check certain categories of FSAVC-buyers to see if they have been 'mis-sold' a policy. However, if you have not heard from them, you will not have been in this category and it is now too late to ask for a review yourself (the closing date was June 2001).

Paying up to £3,600 a year into a stakeholder (or other personal) pension is the third possibility. This has the following advantages:

- you will be able to take part of the pension 'pot' as a lump sum when you retire, which you may not be able to with an AVC or FSAVC;
- with a stakeholder scheme, the charges are controlled and you cannot be penalised for stopping the pension; even for older-style personal pensions, the charges are coming down and should generally be comparable with those for FSAVCs, if not for AVCs; and
- if you move jobs, or lose your job, you can carry on paying into the same policy.

Overall, although AVCs will remain useful for some people, stakeholder pensions will be the preferred choice for many, and FSAVCs seem unlikely to be a good buy for most people.

For more information, see the FSA's *Guide to Topping Up your Occupational Pension*, which is available free from the FSA at the address on page 162.

Earnings above the 'cap'

There is a ceiling on the amount of earnings that can be considered pensionable. This applies to anyone who has moved jobs since 1989, when the cap was introduced. In 2002–2003 it is £97,200. It is possible to make provision for a pension based on the extra earnings by setting up a top-up arrangement without tax relief. But the financial and legal arrangements need to be done properly, so specialist advice should always be taken. You may also be able to negotiate unfunded additional benefits with your employers. Again, these do not carry the same tax privileges as benefits in an ordinary pension scheme.

Working beyond retirement age

If you work beyond retirement age, extra increments can be earned in many occupational pension schemes by deferring the age at which you draw your pension. With a contracted-out earnings-related (COSR) scheme, if you put off drawing your pension for at least seven complete weeks after State Pension age, your Guaranteed Minimum Pension will increase. The amount that earnings-related occupational schemes provide over and above the GMP for late retirement can vary; check your scheme booklet. In a contracted-out money-purchase (COMP) scheme, deferring drawing the pension should mean that the Protected Rights benefit will be increased. The whole pension fund should continue to grow in value. However, there is always the danger that the investment market may continue to stagnate or even fall – perhaps dramatically – so that the value of your fund therefore also declines.

LEAVING AN OCCUPATIONAL PENSION SCHEME

If you leave an employer's pension scheme after having been a member for less than two years, you may be able to take a refund of your contributions, depending on the type of scheme. If it is a contracted-out earnings-related (COSR) scheme, you will receive a refund but 20 per cent tax will be deducted from it, plus the cost of buying you back into SERPS. If it is a contracted-out money-purchase (COMP) scheme, you will not be able to have a refund, but only a preserved or transferred pension. The two-year period includes any pensionable service transferred from a previous pension scheme, and is a rigid limit. If you go one day over, you lose the right to a refund. Nor is a refund permitted if the fund contains transferred rights from an earlier personal pension policy.

For those without the right of refund, there are several choices:

- If you are 50 or over when you leave, you may be offered an immediate pension, reduced to take into account the longer period over which you will receive it.
- Your pension can be 'deferred' or 'preserved' in the existing scheme (see page 64 on the revaluation of preserved earnings-related pensions and page 66 on what happens to preserved money-purchase pensions).
- You have the right to take a transfer. The value of your pension fund can then be transferred to another employer's scheme, if the new trustees allow it, or it can be used to buy a personal pension or a Section 32 'buy-out' bond, as explained below. (See pages 65–66 on how the transfer values of earnings-related pensions are calculated.) There are special rules about the GMP or Protected Rights element of the pension. The trustees of the old scheme are responsible for checking that the policy to which you are transferring meets these.

Section 32 'buy-out' bonds are deferred annuity policies, bought by the trustees from an insurance company chosen by the employee. (An 'annuity' is simply another term for a pension, so a 'deferred annuity' is a pension that is paid to you when you reach retirement age.) Unlike personal pensions, these deferred annuities will match the benefits originally offered in the employer's scheme, such as a Guaranteed Minimum Pension and provision for spouses. This means that you may not have the chance of such high growth in your investment because the money has to be invested cautiously.

You have the right to ask for a transfer out of a scheme at any time up to a year before retirement date. However, the new employer may put on a deadline for acceptance of transfers *in*. For example, in the Teachers' Scheme, you can only transfer pension in from elsewhere within a year of starting in the scheme.

There are a few exceptions to the right to take a transfer:

- If the pension dates from a job change before 1986, and has been fully inflation-proofed since then (as it would have been in the public sector, for example) you can be refused a transfer. However, in general, schemes are happy to offer a transfer in order to get the pension off the books.
- In some cases with older deferred pensions, the scheme rules will only allow you to have a Section 32 buyout (explained above) and not a personal pension.
- If the scheme has already been wound up, and your pension rights have been crystallised into an annuity with an insurance company, you cannot then take a transfer. In most cases, however, you will be offered the chance at an earlier stage, while winding up is still going on.

Earnings-related schemes

If you leave an earnings-related scheme before your pension is due, and you decide to leave your pension where it is, the 'deferred' pension you get at retirement will be calculated on the basis of your salary at leaving, multiplied by the accrual rate and by your years of pensionable service. Part of the deferred pension in contracted-out schemes is the Guaranteed Minimum Pension built up before April 1997 (explained on page 45).

Both this and the remainder of the pension are increased between the date of leaving and the pension date.

Revaluation of preserved pensions

Schemes use different formulae for the GMP increases. The most common in the private sector is a fixed annual rate of increase of 4.5 per cent, compounded over the years until you draw the pension (for anyone leaving after April 2002). Public service schemes index-link the GMP. In all cases, if there is a shortfall in the GMP compared to what would have been your SERPS entitlement at retirement, the State makes up the difference. Alternatively, if the GMP is higher than your SERPS entitlement would have been, it stands still for a few years while SERPS catches up.

The remainder of the pension over and above the GMP also increases, either in line with rises in the Retail Prices Index between the time when you leave and the time when you retire or by 5 per cent compounded over those years, whichever is the lower. (Public service schemes are fully index-linked to prices without the 5 per cent ceiling.) This change only came fully into effect in January 1991, so preserved pensions from earlier job changes may have increases on only part of the pension or none at all.

For that part of the pension that builds up after April 1997, there will be no GMP (as explained on page 46). The whole of the post-1997 part of the pension will increase at 5 per cent a year compound or in line with the Retail Prices Index, whichever is the lower.

The effect of revaluation can be seen in the following example (using, for simplicity, a series of contracted-in schemes):

Example

Jim starts working when he is 25 years old. He leaves his first job after ten years and is then earning £10,000 per year. We assume his salary will increase by 5 per cent a year until he retires. He leaves his second job after ten years with a salary of

---

£16,288. At his third job (another ten-year stint) his leaving salary is £26,532, and the final ten-year stretch brings him up to 65 with a leaving salary of £43,219. As can be seen, with revaluation Jim's pension is increased by around 40 per cent (from £12,004 to £15,603). However, it will not match that earned by people who stay in the same job all their lives, whose whole pension will be based on their final earnings.

	Leaving age	Salary on leaving	After accrual	Preserved pension entitlement	Pension revalued at 2.5%
pa					
Job 1	35	£10,000	$\frac{10}{80}$ =	£1,250	£2,621
Job 2	45	£16,288	$\frac{10}{80}$ =	£2,036	£3,336
Job 3	55	£26,532	$\frac{10}{80}$ =	£3,316	£4,244
Job 4	65	£43,219	$\frac{10}{80}$ =	£5,402	£5,402
			Total	£12,004	£15,603
Total for an employee with 40 continuous years' service =			$\frac{40}{80}$ of	£43,219 =	£21,610

Transfer values

With a final earnings scheme, the transfer value you take elsewhere represents the cost, calculated by the actuary of your old scheme, of buying the deferred pension (explained above) elsewhere. (An actuary is an expert who calculates risks and their financial implications for life assurance companies and pension schemes.) It will vary depending on your age, interest rates, and the assumptions made by the actuary. Although their professional rules (called Guidance Note 11) have largely standardised the calculations and the minimum level is now laid down by law, actuaries still have a considerable amount of discretion, so transfer values vary considerably between schemes.

If the figures are large and you are dissatisfied with the amount of the transfer payment, it may be worth bringing in another pensions professional – probably another actuary – to negotiate on your behalf. This can often be successful, but you will need to pay a fee for the assistance. You can find an actuary through the Association of Consulting Actuaries (address on page 164). If you think there has been maladministration, or a dispute over the facts that have been used in the calculation, you may also wish to go to the Office of the Pensions Advisory Service (OPAS) or the Pensions Ombudsman after raising the issue with the scheme's trustees through the internal disputes procedure, explained on page 141. (See page 163 for the addresses.)

Money-purchase schemes

If you leave a money-purchase scheme, the situation is different. If you decide to leave your pension where it is, the pension will be made 'paid-up', with the charges that have built up so far deducted at this stage. How much these are varies between schemes. With the less good ones, they are quite high and could eat up much of the fund that has built up so far. With the best, there may be no deductions at all. Your pension account then continues to receive the same investment returns as that of any other member, but there will be no further payments into it from either your employer or yourself. The actual pension you get at retirement will be affected by interest rates at the time.

If you take a transfer, it is simply the value of the accumulated fund, after any deductions, that is transferred.

What a transfer buys

In some cases, transferring into a new employer's scheme can buy you extra periods of service within that scheme. In the main public services, for example, there is a 'transfer club' which means that you are given credits according to a standard table used by each scheme. In some cases this will be year for year – that is, if you have ten years' service in the last one you will be counted as having ten years' service in the new scheme. In other cases, the schemes are different; a year's service in one may be counted as rather more, or rather less, than a year in another scheme. In the Teachers' Scheme, for example, the normal retirement age is 60, which means that a pension in it is more valuable than one in the Local Government Pension Scheme (LGPS), where it is 65. So someone transferring from the LGPS to the Teachers' Scheme will receive less than a full year's credited service for each year they transfer.

Importantly, there are time limits on being able to make use of the transfer club. If you miss these and transfer later, you will be offered a much lower amount of credited service. So it is important to keep within the deadlines.

Example

Elsa works for the NHS and builds up 8½ years' service in their scheme. She then goes to work for a local authority and joins their pension scheme. She can bring her 8½ years' credits with her.

In the private sector, however, there is no transfer club. You may be offered extra periods of service in your new employer's scheme, but they will often be fewer than in the previous scheme. This is partly because the benefits in the two schemes will be different. The main reason, however, is that it is expected that your earnings will rise, on average, faster than has been allowed for in the transfer value calculations. You may be offered a money-purchase pension for this element in your new scheme, rather than a pension linked to your earnings.

If you make a transfer into a stakeholder or personal pension or a Section 32 buy-out bond, it will certainly become a money-purchase benefit.

What should you do?

It is impossible to give any definite advice, as so much depends on individual circumstances. The following are a few rules of thumb:

- Be very cautious about taking a transfer of a deferred pension from an earnings-related scheme into a personal pension. You will be swapping a guaranteed benefit for an uncertain one, and also in general paying substantial charges to the company that administers the personal pension (and commission to the person who sells it to you).

- If your scheme is index-linked, such as with a public service scheme, it is even less likely to be wise to transfer into a personal pension scheme.
- It is sometimes sensible to take a transfer across from one earnings-related employer's scheme to another. It all depends on the terms offered. If the new employer is keen for you to take the job, you may be able to bargain for added years in the new scheme.
- It *may* be sensible to transfer between money-purchase schemes, or from a money-purchase scheme to a personal pension. Again, it depends on the terms offered and the charges.

In 1993–94, a major scandal relating to pension transfers was revealed in the financial world. It was estimated that up to half a million people had been 'mis-sold' personal pension transfers when they would have done better to leave their deferred pensions with the old employer. The Treasury and the financial services regulators have now made financial advisers and pension providers check their files. If necessary, they must offer compensation for the pension losses incurred. Some of the sums paid out in settlements are very large, particularly for those who were wrongly transferred from public sector schemes. In some cases, insurance companies have had to pay £20,000–£30,000 per person back into the pension schemes.

If you took out a personal pension between April 1988 and 1994, you should by now have been contacted by those who sold it to you, to ask if you wanted a review. If you refused, it will now be too late to change your mind, unless some new facts have come to light. However, if your case is being reviewed it may be some time before it is finalised. Make sure you keep all the papers safe, and do not ignore any further requests for information.

The Financial Services Authority (FSA) now has tight rules governing those selling pension transfer policies. Before a sale is finalised, you must be sent a 'reasons why' letter explaining precisely why they think that buying a new policy with your transfer value is the right course for you. They should also do a 'transfer value analysis' to show what rate of return you would need in order to benefit. Do not proceed with a transfer without such a letter and analysis, and then only if you feel the reasons are particularly strong.

Whatever you do with the transfer value of your pension, it need not affect your pension choices with your new employer. You could buy a single-premium personal pension policy with it and then start afresh in a new company pension scheme.

For further information, see the FSA's information guide *The Financial Services Authority,* and its *Guide to the Risks of Pension Transfers,* which are available free from the FSA at the address on page 162.

Should you join the new employer's scheme?

For earnings-related schemes, the quick answer is usually yes. Although such schemes vary considerably in quality, the employer will always pay in contributions (over the long term, even if not currently). Not joining, therefore, in effect means giving money back to the employer. Earnings-related schemes also protect your pension against inflation, at least during your working life.

A poor scheme may be improved either by negotiation or by you as an individual putting in AVCs (see pages 56–61). You are also likely to be given additional benefits such as a spouse's pension, a lump-sum death benefit, and a pension if you have to retire because of ill-health.

For money-purchase schemes, again the answer is generally yes. The employer will usually be paying in contributions, and there are normally extra benefits for death and ill-health. The exception might be if the scheme is a low quality COMP (see page 46), with little or nothing extra going in beyond the

National Insurance rebate. Then it could still be worth joining for a younger person, but possibly not for someone old enough to be receiving the maximum National Insurance rebate for contracting out (10.5 per cent from April 2002) because it is not intended to compensate in full for the lost S2P pension.

The official regulatory bodies take the view that there would need to be a very good reason for someone with an employer's scheme (earnings-related or money-purchase) available to them to buy a personal or stakeholder pension instead. The only group for whom this might not be true are people who are sure they will stay less than two years with the employer (for example those on short-term contracts).

However, no one has to join an employer's scheme. Your other options are to rely on S2P or to take out a personal or stakeholder pension. As already pointed out, S2P on its own will not produce a good retirement income although it will provide a better deal than SERPS for those on low to moderate pay. So the real choice is between an employer's scheme, if available, and a personal pension. Personal pensions are described in detail in the next chapter; their advantages and disadvantages are summarised on pages 90–91. Stakeholder pensions are explained on pages 92–94.

● If your employer's scheme is contracted in, you could take out a rebate-only appropriate personal pension in place of S2P, while still paying into the employer's scheme. As explained on pages 77–78, this is wise only if you are below a certain age and reasonably well paid.

For more information, see the *FSA Guide to the Risks of Opting Out of your Employer's Pension Scheme.*

If your employer changes

Over the past few years, many people have found that their job has remained the same but the employer has changed, perhaps because of a takeover or because of the contracting out of services in the public sector.

The legal position here is quite complex, because pensions are not covered by the Transfer of Undertakings (Protection of Employment) Regulations which protect other conditions of employment, although the DTI has been consulting about extending the regulations to cover them. On the other hand, there may be alternative contractual protection. To play safe, public sector employers and many larger private ones insist that the new employer offer equivalent (but not identical) pension benefits to transferred employees. It will then almost always be worth joining the new scheme for future service. The decision on whether to transfer past service across will depend on the terms offered – you may need independent financial advice on this. If you are a member of a trade union or staff association, it should be able to assist with negotiating the arrangements here. (See pages 144–145 for more details on this.)

In a few cases, such as local government and teaching, a new employer may be able to arrange for you to stay with the existing scheme. There are also a few schemes which cover more than one employer in the same industry – such as the Railways Pension Scheme for those working for the different railway companies.

EARLY RETIREMENT

How much you can get on early retirement under an employer's pension scheme varies enormously. Unless the retirement is due to ill-health (see below), you will not in any case be able to draw the employer's pension before you are 50. It will then be worked out taking into account the number of years you have been a member of the scheme and your earnings at retirement or the size of the fund available in a money-purchase scheme. If you are taking early retirement at the employer's request – really a form of redundancy – or if you are suffering from ill-health, you may be given credits for some or all of your prospective years of service (the period up to retirement when you could have worked but are not going to).

It may be possible for you to arrange for a lump sum to go into the pension scheme from your employer, to increase your pension, with an equivalent cut in a severance or redundancy payment. Ask the pensions administrator or HR department if this could be arranged.

In other cases, however – especially if you are retiring at your own request – you may find that the early retirement pension is very small. It could be reduced well below its normal amount, because of an 'actuarial reduction'. This is designed to spread the same amount of pension over a longer period. The figures used vary; the reduction could be 6 per cent for each year of early retirement, for example.

Example

Ahmed decides to retire at 60. His scheme has a retirement age of 65, but his pension is calculated only on the years of service he has actually worked, up to 60. It is then reduced by 30 per cent, ie 6 per cent for each year that he could have worked, if he had carried on to the company's normal retirement age.

At worst, you may not be allowed to draw a pension at all, if most of it consists of Guaranteed Minimum Pension (explained on page 45). The law says that there must be enough in the scheme to pay the proper GMP entitlement when you reach retirement age. If you are paid some pension early, there might not be enough. So in some schemes, the whole pension is held back to make sure.

On the other hand, a better employer should be willing to add to your pension so that there is enough in the fund for you to draw some pension early without harming the later GMP. Check your scheme booklet to see what is on offer. If it does not seem very good, ask your union or staff association to try to negotiate a better deal. Insist on a statement in writing of what you will get before committing yourself to early retirement.

You may find that there are restrictions on taking other employment once you have started drawing the pension, especially in the public sector.

Final salary schemes can be very flexible over early retirement, especially if there is a surplus on the fund (explained on pages 143–144) which means that extra money for a particular case can be found without harming the rest. However, early retirements can be very expensive, because it means less has come in as contributions and the pension will be paid for a longer time than if you worked on to normal retirement date. So some schemes, especially in the public sector, have made early retirement much less easily available recently than it used to be.

Ill-health retirement

If you are too sick to work, then you will usually need to apply to the trustees of the scheme for ill-health retirement. In some schemes, however, it is the employer who takes the decision and tells the trustees what to do. Whoever takes the decision should do so after taking proper medical advice.

If you think you have not been fairly treated, check the procedures and definitions of 'ill-health' (it might be called 'invalidity' or 'incapacity' in your scheme) laid down in the trust deed. Every scheme has to have an internal disputes procedure (explained on page 141) so if you are dissatisfied you should take your case through that, if necessary with the help of OPAS.

Terminal illness

Many scheme rules say that, if someone is terminally ill, the whole of the pension can be commuted into a lump sum, although some tax will be paid on it.

Early retirement and AVCs

After a recent change in the Inland Revenue's rules, it is now possible to start taking whatever pension you can buy from your AVCs, before you start to draw the main pension. This right is probably only theoretical, however, as for most people the AVC pension on its own would not be enough to live on.

Deferred pensions from other employers

If you have worked for other employers in the past, and have left deferred pensions with them, you may also be able to ask for them to be paid early. However, they will probably be heavily reduced. Ask the trustees of your former schemes for details of what you would get, and of what their policy is.

Personal Pensions

A personal pension can be bought by almost anyone, including people with no earnings, employed and self-employed people without another pension scheme, and (within some limits) people who are also paying into an occupational pension.

For self-employed people, who cannot contribute towards a SERPS pension or an employer's scheme, paying into a personal pension is the only way they can increase their pension benefits over and above the State Basic Pension.

This chapter looks at the different types of personal pension available, including appropriate personal pensions, Section 226 policies and single-premium pensions. It also looks at the different types of annuity you might buy when you draw your pension and ways of increasing your pension. Stakeholder pensions, almost all of which are a special type of personal pension, are considered in a special section.

HOW PERSONAL PENSION SCHEMES WORK

● Stakeholder pensions are a special type of personal pension. The differences between them and ordinary personal pensions are dealt with on pages 92–94.

You can buy (or have bought for you) a personal pension at any age from 0 until your 75th birthday, whether you have any earnings or not, although if you belong to an employer's pension scheme there are special rules about buying a personal pension in addition. You can draw your pension any time between the ages of 50 and 75.

Personal pensions are always money-purchase, and the Inland Revenue imposes limits on what can go in rather than what can come out in pension form. If you have been putting money into the personal pension yourself, when you draw your pension you can receive part of the accumulated pension fund built up from that as a tax-free lump sum – usually 25 per cent. The rest of the fund is used to buy an annuity (see pages 95–103), which will provide you with an income for the rest of your life.

There are two types of personal pension – those that are 'appropriate' (for contracting out of SERPS/S2P) and those that are not. Before 1988, personal pensions could not be used to contract out of SERPS and the rules were different. At that time they were called 'Section 226' policies or 'retirement annuities' (see page 90). People who already have these have been allowed to retain them and continue paying in, but no new ones have been started since 1988.

Personal pensions can be offered by banks, building societies or other financial institutions, but the most usual choice is an insurance company.

Appropriate personal pensions

An appropriate personal pension (APP) allows you as an individual to contract out of SERPS, and since April 2002 from the new S2P. You and your employer pay National Insurance contributions at the full rate, but the National Insurance Contributions Office (NICO) then pays over the National Insurance rebate (see page 15), plus tax relief on the employee's share of the rebate, directly to your personal pension provider. These rebates are 'age-related', rising to 10.5 per cent of your relevant earnings (more than your National Insurance contributions) for someone currently aged 48 or over. The maximum limits on contributions explained on page 86 are on top of these age-related payments.

The fund that builds up from this part of your contributions is described as your Protected Rights. The money in the Protected Rights part of an APP normally has to be paid as an annuity and not as a lump sum. It has to be paid at the same rate to men and women of the same age. (Insurance companies are not required apart from this to offer equal annuity rates for women and men, and choose not to do so because of women's longer average life expectancy.) It also has to include a spouse's pension and provision for a 3 per cent increase each year for pension from contributions made before April 1997, or by 5 per cent for each year – or in line with the Retail Prices Index, if less – for pension from contributions made after that date.

APPs can be taken out by any employee who is not contracted out of S2P through an employer's pension scheme. So this includes both people who do not belong to a scheme at all, and those who belong to a scheme which is contracted in (see page 44). In this second case, however, only the money from the NI rebate can go into the APP.

Self-employed people do not belong to S2P to start with, as explained on page 9, and cannot therefore contract out with an APP.

How age and earnings affect the APP decision

As explained on pages 47–49, one crucial factor that determines how much pension you get from any money-purchase scheme is the age at which your contributions go in. For younger people, the investment returns on the National Insurance rebate may well give them a pension better than the S2P contributions they are giving up; for people in their late 40s or early 50s they may well not do so, even with age-related rebates.

Another important issue is how much you earn, and how much you will be contributing to your pension fund. The financial institutions offering personal pensions have to pay their overheads and make a profit. So they make deductions from the contributions to cover their expenses. Since it costs nearly as much to administer a small pension fund as a large one, these deductions have tended in the past to be flat-rate, or heavily weighted against small contributors. Lower-paid people have lost proportionately more, and found it more difficult to acquire an APP that offers a better return than SERPS/S2P.

However, the level of insurance companies' charges, and their structure, is changing as they face up to the new challenge of stakeholder pensions (see pages 92–94). Since these are lower-cost and have a very simple charging structure, providers have had to cut and simplify their charges to match. It is more likely now, therefore, that a low-paid person will be able to find a personal pension to suit them than it would have been a few years ago.

Women on the whole get a poorer deal out of personal pensions than men. Annuity rates for women are lower for women because of their longer life expectancy (although the Protected Rights element of an APP has to be paid at the same rate to men and women of the same age). The other side of this is that women will get a better deal out of S2P because they draw it for longer. To limit the risks, one answer is to have a personal pension on top of S2P, rather than an APP, as explained below.

Personal pensions on top of S2P

The second type of personal pension loses the adjective 'appropriate' because they are not contracted out of S2P. For employees, they sit on top of S2P rather than replacing it.

People who take out this type of personal pension get tax relief on their contributions but no NI rebate payments. Tax relief at the basic rate is given directly by the Inland Revenue to the pension provider, but the higher-rate element has to be claimed (see pages 83–85 for details of the tax relief).

You can pay a lump-sum single premium for a personal pension policy in any year. There is then no further commitment to stick with that provider, and in future years you can shop around for the best arrangement. (At retirement you will usually be able to put the proceeds of all the policies together to buy a single annuity.)

Alternatively, you can sign a contract to pay regular premiums to one pension provider, on a monthly, quarterly or annual basis. This ties you to that contract, and you can find you are penalised if you stop it early.

When you retire, you can take up to 25 per cent of your pension fund as a tax-free lump sum, and use the rest of the fund to buy yourself an annuity. An annuity is simply a pension paid for life. It may end with your death or, if you have a surviving spouse, carry on until his or her death. It can remain level or increase each year. The more 'extras' of this sort you add in, the lower the starting amount will be. The different types of annuity you can buy are discussed on pages 97–102.

Your retirement income with a personal pension therefore depends on:

- the length of time the money has been invested;
- how good the investment returns were;
- how much you paid in management and commission charges;
- annuity rates when you start to draw the pension; and
- what type of annuity you choose.

The timing can make a lot of difference: interest rates change not only from year to year but often overnight, and they will affect the lifelong returns on any annuity. The higher annuity rates are when it begins, the bigger the annuity will be in return for the lump sum you have paid for it. The other side of this, however, is that when interest rates come down (as they have in the last few years) the annuity will be smaller for the same lump sum. For example, according to the Annuity Bureau, in June 1995 a 65-year-old couple with a £100,000 pension fund could have bought a joint life annuity of £9,546 a year, whereas today the same sum of money would buy them only £6,812.

In addition, life expectancy for pensioners – or at least for those who have a reasonable income to live on – is going up. Most of us would view this as a good thing, of course, but it does mean that the same sum of money has to be spread over a longer period. So this too is increasing the cost of future annuities.

These factors, taken together, make it likely that many people are not paying enough towards their personal pensions to ensure that they have a comfortable retirement. It is important to keep an eye on one's fund, and what it will buy, so that corrective action can be taken before it is too late.

Types of personal pension policy

There are a number of different types of personal pension policy on the market. Any of these can be 'appropriate' (for contracting out) or non-appropriate.

Deposit-based policies

These are very similar to ordinary savings accounts. Your contributions are saved for you until retirement and earn a variable interest rate for the time when the money is on deposit. There is not usually a penalty for stopping and starting contributions, or for beginning to draw the pension earlier than you originally envisaged, but the returns may well be lower than for other forms of policy.

With-profits policies

The traditional type of insurance policy is the 'with-profits' one where bonuses are added during the lifetime of the policy and cannot then be taken away.

There will also be a final 'terminal' bonus when you draw your pension.

With some older with-profits policies, an underlying guaranteed rate of return was written into the contract at the time you took out the contract. These guarantees were seen as a sales device, and the insurance companies do not seem to have expected that they would ever come into force. Faced with extra costs, therefore, some insurance companies said that you would only receive the benefit of a guarantee if the terminal bonus is reduced as an offset. This policy was challenged in the courts in the case of Equitable Life, with disastrous results for the company when it lost. There are still question marks over the way some other insurance companies are administering their guarantees.

If you have an existing with-profits policy, look at the small print of the contract to see if you are covered by a guarantee. If so, think carefully about giving up or altering the policy (and take advice) as you are unlikely to be able to replace the guarantee with anything better.

Unitised with-profits policies link the value of the policy to units in a fund. Generally, annual bonuses are also provided which cannot be taken away once granted. There is however at least one 'with-profits' policy on sale where the policy rules do allow for the value to be reduced as well as increased, so check the small print.

Unit-linked policies

With this type, your contributions are invested in unit trusts or unit-linked insurance policies, after a deduction for commission and expenses. With unit trusts your money is paid into a pool, from which investment managers buy a range of stocks and shares. Your pension fund at any time will depend on the value of the units at that time. It can therefore go down in value as well as up.

Which to choose?

Deposit-based and with-profits policies give a more predictable return than unit-linked policies, but with both unit-linked and with-profits policies much depends on the investment performance of the pension fund. Tables of past returns appear in such publications as *Money Management*, *MoneyFacts* and *Money Marketing*, and current annuity rates are given in *Pensions World* and elsewhere. Future returns can only be an estimate, and research for the Financial Services Authority suggests that the past is a very poor guide to the future.

Many unit-linked pension policies were not launched until the 1980s, and deposit-based ones much later, so direct comparison with the traditional with-profits policies is not always possible. The best unit-linked companies have done better than the best with-profits ones, but the worst have done very poorly indeed. The situation is complicated, however, by the fact that many insurance companies have been using their reserves to keep up the level of bonuses on with-profits policies. Some are now in danger of using up their reserves, and most have been cutting back on the level of bonuses.

Unit-linked and with-profits policies are meant for the longer haul; of the two, unit-linked policies are less predictable, with-profits policies more stable. Deposit-based policies make safe havens for people nearing retirement who want to consolidate or preserve the pension that has already built up for them, perhaps in a unit-linked fund.

Switching investments

The standard advice for people approaching retirement is to consolidate past investment gains. This means gradually switching your pension fund out of share-based investments into less volatile investments like bonds or gilts.

Most unit-linked personal pensions have a wide range of investment options offering different degrees of investment risk. Some will automatically switch you out of high-risk investments during the last few years before retirement in what is often called a 'lifestyle' arrangement. If your policy does not have an automatic switching facility, ask the adviser who sold you the policy for advice on how and when to switch. There may be a charge for switching, but many policies allow you at least one free switch each year.

Tax rules for personal pensions

These changed considerably after April 2001 so as to allow many more people to pay contributions. The rules are now:

- If you are not in an occupational scheme (see below for the rules about these), you will be able to pay £3,600 a year (including the basic-rate tax relief given by the Inland Revenue) into a personal pension whether you are earning or not, and without needing to prove how much you are earning.
- If your earnings fluctuate, or if you have stopped work and therefore stopped earning, you can pay a contribution based on your best earnings figure within the last five years (see page 84).

The maximum proportion of your 'net relevant earnings' that you are allowed to pay into a personal pension rises as you get older. Net relevant earnings are total earnings for employees. For the self-employed they are their earnings less some of the deductions allowed for tax purposes.

Age at 6 April each year	Percentage of net relevant earnings that can be paid in to a personal pension that year
under 35	17.5
36–45	20.0
46–50	25.0
51–55	30.0
56–60	35.0
61–74	40.0

(Note: This is *on top* of the National Insurance rebate for contracting out with an appropriate personal pension.)

Howard stops work at 56, having received pay of £25,000 in his final year. So if he wishes (and has the money), he can pay 35 per cent of £25,000 (£8,750) per year into his personal pension during that tax year and for the following five tax years. After that, if he still wishes to continue paying, he will have to drop down to the £3,600 level, however.

Important points for anyone who has (or is thinking of) a personal pension are:

- 10 per cent of the total contribution can be used to pay for life insurance.
- It is possible to put shares from an approved employee share scheme into your pension fund and attract tax relief. (However, many advisers would warn against this, as it could mean putting too many eggs in one basket. If the company collapsed, your pension would suffer too.)
- You can also have tax relief on 'waiver of contributions' arrangements (explained on page 86).
- If you belong to an occupational pension scheme (except one that has changed its tax status, as explained on page 44), are not a controlling director and earn no more than £30,000 a year, you will be able to put £3,600 (including the basic-rate tax relief) a year into a personal pension as well as anything going into your employer's scheme.

The Inland Revenue's rules on calculating the earning on which to base contributions, for the purpose of their maximum limits, have been made very flexible. You have to nominate a particular tax year as the 'basis year'. This can be either the current one, or any of the previous five, and this then gives you a contribution limit for this tax year. You can continue to use this same 'basis year' for any of the next five years, or you can move forward to another 'basis year' that gives you a better result.

So this means, for example, that if you earn more in 2001–2002 than in 2002–2003, you can use the former as the 'basis year' for your contributions for the next few years. On the other hand, if 2003–2004 turns out to be a better year for you, you can re-base your earnings on 2001–2002, and use that for another five years.

On the other hand, if you are in an occupational scheme and have earnings this year just below the £30,000 figure, you can choose to use this figure for the next five years to allow you to put money into a personal pension as well as your occupational scheme.

You will see that the top limits are higher than for employees' contributions to an occupational pension scheme, but on the other hand many employers make no contributions to their employees' personal or stakeholder pensions. If the employer does contribute, it must be set against this limit.

Since 1989 there has also been an absolute limit on the amount of contributions going into personal pension schemes. There is a maximum earnings figure of £97,200 in 2002–2003 above which you can no longer put in the maximum percentage appropriate to your age. This figure is known as the 'earnings cap' and rises each year in line with the Retail Prices Index.

Protection for dependants

In an appropriate personal pension scheme, the Protected Rights benefits must include a pension for the protected widow or protected widower in the event of the member's death, but this will often be very small. It is also usual to pay over the balance of the fund that has built up from the member's contributions, with or without interest. With any type of personal pension, you need to pay extra premiums if you want to provide life assurance for dependants in the form of a lump sum or a larger continuing pension.

Tax relief is allowed on life assurance premiums of up to 10 per cent of the premium, within the limits for total contributions to a personal pension scheme.

As an example, a 49-year-old man might expect to pay around £25 per month to get life assurance of £50,000 until his retirement age of 65. A woman might pay between £12 and £14 monthly for the same sum up to the age of 60. Lower premiums will give a smaller sum on death.

If you later decide to join an occupational pension scheme and therefore to stop your personal pension, life assurance linked with your personal pension will lapse at the same time as you make that policy paid up. You would be able to continue it without the tax relief, but this may not be necessary as most occupational schemes provide a reasonable level of death benefits as part of the package (see page 49).

Ill-health

You may be able to draw your pension early on grounds of ill-health, but some providers penalise you heavily for this. With many personal pensions set up before 6 April 2001 a 'waiver' of premium is allowed if you become ill or disabled before 60 or 65. This means that your contributions continue to be paid for as long as you are not earning due to ill-health.

The rules on this changed in April 2001. For policies taken out after that date, a 'waiver benefit' cannot be included in the policy, but you can buy separate insurance to carry on the contributions in both sickness and unemployment. Tax relief will be given when those contributions are paid into the personal pension. Few of these policies are being sold, however, and it may be better value to buy a general 'income protection' policy which gives you control over what you spend the income from the insurance company on, rather than one where the income can only be spent on pension contributions.

You may be able to obtain State benefits if you become unable to work because of disability or sickness, as explained on pages 29–32.

For information on all State benefits, see Age Concern Books annual publication *Your Rights*.

Charges

It is important to look at the charges when taking out a personal pension policy. These cover the provider's costs in setting up the scheme, commission and other payments to those selling you the scheme, and the provider's profits.

As with all consumer purchases, you must shop around and do your research to get the best value for money. The wrong choice will cost you thousands of pounds.

Getting advice

You can buy a personal pension policy in one of two ways: either direct from an insurance company or financial institution or its 'appointed representative'; or via an independent financial adviser. If you buy direct from appointed representatives, at present they can only sell the products of that particular provider (although they still have an obligation to tell you if these products are unsuitable for you). Legally, independent advisers must give you 'best advice' about all the policies on the market, on the basis of what is best for you rather than what pays the highest commission. This is called 'polarisation' and these rules are in the process of being altered, as explained on page 149.

For more information about the different types of financial adviser, and about making sure that you get good financial advice, see pages 146–150. The level of commission payable has to be disclosed to purchasers, and you should look carefully at these figures. You may be able to negotiate lower commission in some circumstances.

An alternative is to go to an independent adviser who charges a fee rather than taking commission if a policy is bought (see page 148 for details).

Regular premiums or single premiums?

You can sign a contract to pay regular premiums into a personal pension scheme over a number of years, or you can pay separate single premiums each year, either to the same provider or to different ones, as you wish. Unless you feel you need the discipline of the contract, it usually makes more sense to pay single premiums. This results in lower initial charges, and also gives you the freedom to switch providers. It could mean that you end up with a whole sheaf of individual policies, but when you draw your pension you will have the option of putting them together into one or buying a number of different annuities.

The Financial Services Authority warned in the run-up to the launch of stakeholder pensions that providers should be careful about selling policies that will be difficult to change for a stakeholder pension when these came on stream. In response, many firms offered 'pre-stakeholder' guarantees, some of which were more valuable than others. If you bought a personal pension between 1998 and 2001, check whether the policy carried such a guarantee, what it really means and what you have to do to bring it into effect. If there is no guarantee, ask the advisers to explain (in writing) why in their view it was 'best advice' to take out this policy.

'Group' personal pensions

'Group' personal pensions (GPPs) are sold by insurance companies to employers who do not want to go to the trouble of setting up a company pension scheme. At their most basic, all they mean is that the employer makes an arrangement with a particular adviser or insurance company so that they sell individual personal pensions to employees during work-time. The employer may 'facilitate' by offering to deduct contributions from your pay at source if you sign up for that package. Sometimes the charges to the individual are no lower than if you bought the policy yourself, but sensible employers will negotiate a better deal to reflect the fact that they are doing much of the work.

The better GPPs also include a substantial extra contribution from the employer, and automatic provision of a lump-sum death benefit and insurance against ill-health.

The rules for stakeholder pensions (explained on pages 92–94) say that if employers already have a GPP for all their staff to which they contribute at least 3 per cent of pay, and where there are no penalties for leaving, they need not offer stakeholder pensions to their employees.

If you are offered a GPP to which the employer is making a contribution, matching your own or better, it is probably good advice to take it up. But if the employer is putting in less than this, or if you already have a personal pension which you would be penalised for giving up, it is important that you take independent advice. It would generally be best to do this on a fee-paying basis (see page 148), as it is unlikely that the adviser would be able to sell you another insurance product from which they could receive commission. There are penalties on employers for not paying the members' and their own contributions across quickly, as there are for occupational pensions (see page 139).

Self-invested pension plans

Self-invested pension plans (SIPPs) are personal pensions where the policyholders own the investments. You build up a portfolio of investments out of which your pension will be provided, rather than leaving the pension provider to make the investments. SIPPs are for the richer and more sophisticated investors who can afford the relatively high setting-up costs. However, these fees are fixed, so there should be no hidden charges.

The investment and administrative functions of SIPPs are separated (whereas in other personal pensions you buy a package deal). You can therefore switch investment managers as well as or instead of the actual investments. This can be very important for people in professional partnerships and similar managerial positions. The usual range of investments is available. However, SIPPs have penalties as well as advantages. Take professional advice before setting one up.

Section 226 policies

Before 1988, self-employed people and those not in an employer's scheme were able to take out personal pension policies known as Section 226 retirement annuity policies. These are no longer available, but if you have one or more you are allowed to keep them going.

In some cases, you can draw a larger lump sum from a Section 226 policy than the 25 per cent maximum allowed with a personal pension. On the other hand, Section 226 policies do not allow you to draw a pension before the age of 60, whereas with personal pensions the earliest age is 50.

You can transfer a Section 226 policy into a personal pension if you are anxious to get the money earlier and if the insurer allows you to, but it means sacrificing part of the lump sum. You may also be able to alter your policy if its original terms no longer suit you – for example to provide larger death benefits and a smaller pension. This will depend on the terms of your policy. Make sure you get advice before doing this.

Advantages and disadvantages of personal pensions

Advantages

- They are portable: you suffer no loss if you change jobs but carry on paying in.
- The only limits are on contributions, which depend on your age and current or past earnings. Within these limits, there is no restriction on the size of your individual pension fund, so advantage can be taken of stock market conditions to improve fund growth.
- You are free to choose your policy provider and may be able to switch providers if you wish.
- The lump sum at retirement could be greater than from an earnings-related scheme – if you have paid in enough money and achieved a good investment return.
- You may be able to contract out of S2P with the age-related rebate (taking out an appropriate personal pension).

Disadvantages

- Retirement benefit levels are not guaranteed. The final pay-out depends on annuity rates and the investment performance of your pension fund, less commission and administration charges.
- Extra benefits such as those for death or ill-health will cost you extra.
- Employers do not usually contribute to personal pensions (except the better GPPs), so less will generally be paid into them, leading to lower benefits.
- If you subsequently want to join or rejoin your present employer's scheme (earnings-related or money-purchase), you may not be allowed to do so or it may be on less favourable terms.
- Commission paid to the person who sells you the personal pension is generally deducted from the investment fund into which your contributions go. This may be a substantial amount.
- Administration charges are made by the personal pension provider and may absorb a large proportion of the contributions paid. They will bear more heavily on the lower paid with smaller pension funds.
- Owing to commission and administration charges, many personal pensions will be poor value if held for only a short time, and some will be poor value even if held for longer.

- **The Financial Services Authority's website (www.fsa.gov.uk) includes a set of comparative tables so that you can see the effect that different insurance companies' charges will have on your final pension.**

STAKEHOLDER PENSIONS

Stakeholder pensions are a special sort of personal pension, which the Government has targeted at those earning between about £10,800 and £24,600 who are not in an occupational pension scheme. They began in April 2001, with two important features:

- legal requirements on employers to give people access to a scheme through the workplace, and to make deductions from pay and pass them on; and
- strict government regulation on what can be charged.

However, employers are *not* required to contribute to stakeholder schemes.

The main details of stakeholder pensions are:

- A percentage of each individual's fund (no more than 1 per cent a year) is deducted by those running the scheme, to cover all normal operating costs. Extra charges for extra services such as individual advice will be allowed, but the customer must have the option of not taking these services.
- The minimum contribution level must be no higher than £20, and there must be no minimum frequency of contributions.
- There must be no charges or penalties for transfers, and stakeholder schemes must accept transfers from other schemes.

Access via the employer

Although it is possible to buy them in other ways, the main way in which people sign up for stakeholder pensions is through the workplace. If the employer has five or more employees, it must provide a stakeholder scheme, within three months of starting work, if there is not an occupational scheme that employees are entitled to join after a waiting period of up to a year. The occupational scheme is also allowed to exclude those aged under 18 or within five years of starting retirement.

Group Personal Pensions can also exempt the employer from providing access to a stakeholder scheme, so long as the employer is contractually committed to make a contribution of 3 per cent or more of basic pay and the individual will not be penalised for stopping payments into the scheme. The employer can require the individual to make a contribution to the GPP as well, but cannot insist that this is more than 3 per cent of basic pay. However, if the scheme was set up before 8 October 2001 (the start date for these rules), the employer can make it a condition that the employee contributes at a higher level than this, but not at a higher rate than the employer does. So, for example, a scheme which already existed before October 2001 could have an employer contribution of 8 per cent and an employee contribution of 4 per cent, and still provide exemption for the employer.

'Access' means that the employer 'designates' a scheme. You can then ask the employer then to make a deduction from your pay, and pass the money over to that designated scheme within a time limit. If an employer changes the designated scheme, it must continue to pass on contributions to the old one if the employees want it to. An employer is not required, however, to pass on contributions to any other scheme, so if you want to deal with a different provider, you will need to make some other arrangement, such as a direct debit.

Where the employer is making the deductions, individuals will only be able to change their contribution levels every six months at most, although they can always insist that their contributions are stopped immediately.

Stakeholder schemes are regulated by the Occupational Pensions Regulatory Authority (Opra) (see page 138), as with occupational schemes. The people selling them have to follow rules laid down by the Financial Services Authority (see page 146), as with personal pensions. Details of the FSA's requirements on the selling of stakeholder pensions are included in its Conduct of Business rules.

The Government thinks that most people should be able to reach decisions on which pension to take out without individual advice, so long as the literature is clear and there are flow-charts and 'decision-trees' available (explained on page 147). So it is only possible for providers or IFAs to charge above the 1 per cent limit explained above if there is extra advice to be given.

A few stakeholder pension schemes, including the one being run by the TUC particularly for trade union members, are 'trust based', and the rules say that they must have one-third independent trustees (see pages 138–139 for an explanation of what trustees do). Most schemes, however, are contract-based, and run by large insurance companies or other commercial providers. Stakeholder providers are entitled to say that you cannot pay your contributions in cash, but they cannot restrict you to other payment methods like the Internet or direct debit. Most will try to persuade people to use the Internet for all contact with them, however.

Finding out more about stakeholder pensions

There are plenty of leaflets, telephone helplines, and websites around covering stakeholder pensions. The DWP has a leaflet called *A Guide to Your Pension Options*, and another one called *Stakeholder Pensions: Your guide*. You can order these by phoning 0845 731 3233.

The FSA has a factsheet called *Stakeholder Pensions and Decision Trees*, which you can use to go through the question of whether a stakeholder pension is right for you. The FSA's consumer helpline is on 0845 606 1234.

The Government has paid for a helpline for the public to ring to find out more, the number for which is 0845 601 2923. Calls are charged at local rates, and the line is open between 8.30am–6.30pm, Monday to Friday. However, the helpline cannot provide specific financial advice.

The Occupational Pensions Regulatory Authority (Opra) has a website (www.stakeholder.opra.gov.uk) which has links leading you through to other official sites and also to the register of all the different providers and to the providers' own websites.

DRAWING YOUR PENSION

When you draw a personal pension, certain choices are open to you. You can choose whether to take the maximum permitted lump sum and you can also choose which type of annuity to buy and which company to buy it from. This gives you a range of options in respect of retirement benefits.

The lump sum

With a personal pension, the maximum part of your pension fund that may be taken as a tax-free lump sum is usually 25 per cent. The Protected Rights element in an appropriate personal pension (APP – see pages 76–77) must be used to buy a pension. This may limit your lump sum to less than the maximum allowed. With one of the older Section 226 policies it could be more, but if you want to purchase your annuity from a company other than the one which issued your original Section 226 contract, it may limit the lump sum payable to 25 per cent. Unless there is a huge disparity in the annuity rates offered, people usually stay with the policy that gives the larger lump sum because of the tax advantage.

Taking the largest possible tax-free lump sum tends to be a better choice than taking the whole amount as taxable pension income, both because of the tax advantage and because it gives you more options.

Buying an annuity

Most of the money built up in a personal pension fund must be used to buy an annuity, which provides your retirement income. By law, only insurance companies, and not other personal pension providers, can provide annuities. Once you have bought your annuity the payments from the insurance company will continue whatever happens, within the terms of the contract.

It is possible to use your tax-free lump sum to purchase an additional annuity. This can have tax advantages as part of the payment is treated as a return of your own capital and is therefore tax-free, but most people prefer to keep the money.

Annuity rates vary with age. The younger you are when you purchase an annuity, the less income you will get; the older you are, the bigger the income. Annuity rates for women are lower than for men (except for the Protected Rights element, where rates must be equal) because women's longer average life expectancy means that they are likely to be paid the income for longer. This practice is allowed under the Sex Discrimination Act.

As explained on pages 99–100, annuity rates also depend on current interest rates, and on the predictions of life expectancy.

With an appropriate personal pension (APP), the Protected Rights element has to go into an annuity that increases by 3 per cent each year and carries with it a widow's or widower's pension also. (Pension you build up from 6 April 1997 must increase by 5 per cent each year or in line with the Retail Prices Index.) With a personal pension, and the extra money in an APP over and above the Protected Rights element, there is no such requirement, and you can choose how to arrange the benefits. You can also normally choose your annuity if you have a Section 226 policy, a SIPP or an FSAVC.

You do not have to buy your annuity from the pension provider to whom you have paid your pension contributions. You will have an 'open market option' (OMO) which allows you to choose any insurance company where the annuity rates may be better. Your original pension provider normally provides the tax-free lump sum, and the rest of your pension fund is then transferred at retirement under a 'substitution contract' to provide your pension. However, your existing provider may penalise you for moving or offer a 'loyalty bonus' for staying, which comes to much the same thing.

Annuity rates vary considerably between providers, so you could improve your pension by up to 30 per cent by shopping around in this way. However, there may also be a fee or commission to pay to your adviser, so taking up the OMO may not be worthwhile if you have only a small fund. (One adviser puts the breakpoint at around £50,000.) It will almost always be worth enquiring about this, perhaps with one of the specialist IFAs who deals with annuities, even if you do not go ahead.

You can draw income directly from your fund, up until the year you are 75, rather than taking an annuity. This is called 'income drawdown' and is dealt with on pages 103–105.

Which type of annuity?

The right choice of annuity can affect your retirement income considerably, as well as your peace of mind. An independent financial adviser (see page 146) should be able to 'shop around' for you and find the best value available at the time. (See page 149 on how to make sure you are given good advice.) However, you will get better advice if you have worked out your requirements already.

From September 2002 onwards, all providers have to inform consumers of their right to shop around for the best annuity rate (the OMO) well in advance of their retirement date. Insurance companies should also explain the different types of annuity available, under their own code of good practice. From Spring 2003 onwards, the FSA will be publishing comparative tables of annuity rates, which will make it easier for consumers to shop around.

There are a number of different types of annuities, and several new types have come on the market in the last few years. The Treasury has been consulting on various changes to the rules it lays down, although none of them are very radical.

Retirement income products

	Non-investment linked annuities
Flat annuity	Provides a fixed level of income for life, but does not increase over time.
Escalating annuity	Fixed annual rises at, for example, 3% or 5%, without investment risk.
RPI-linked annuity	Rises linked to the RPI, without investment risk.
Limited price indexed annuity	A RPI link but capped (often at 5%), without investment risk.
Dependant's benefits	Provides income after the pensioner's death for a spouse or dependent children.
Guaranteed period annuities	Promises to pay the annuity for a predetermined period of up to 10 years, whether the pensioner survives or not.
Impaired life annuities	Provides higher annuities for people with certain medical conditions limiting their life expectancy.
	Investment-linked products
With-profits annuity	Two components – guaranteed minimum and bonuses. Requires the annuitant to choose a quite complex assumed bonus rate (ABR).
Unit-linked annuities with investment choices, eg high, medium or tracker	Generally regarded as high risk, but still different degrees of risk depending on investment choices.
Drawdown	Highest risk.

(Source: *Modernising Annuities: A consultative document –* Inland Revenue, February 2002)

Annuities that are not linked to investment return

Once you have bought an annuity not linked to the returns on the capital invested, the terms are fixed. There are choices to be made before you buy:

- Do you want a high starting level that remains fixed for the rest of your life or a lower one that increases by a percentage each year? (If you want a pension linked to the Retail Prices Index, the starting level will be lower still.)
- Do you want a guarantee that the pension will be paid for a minimum length of time – perhaps five or ten years?
- Do you want the pension for yourself alone or do you want it to continue until your spouse's death (called a 'joint-life and survivor' pension)?
- Do you want to get a slightly higher rate in return for taking your income 12 months in arrears, or do you prefer to play for safety and get very much less in return for being paid a year in advance?
- Do you want payments monthly or quarterly?

All these options are possible, and will affect the income you get from your annuity. Other factors such as interest rates and your age, health and sex will also affect it.

It is also possible to get a better rate if you fall into a special category – such as being a lifelong smoker. Since this reduces your life expectancy, there are insurance companies which offer higher annuity rates. For example one quote (1 June 2002) was for an extra £656.64 per year, from a fund of £100,000. Similarly, if you are an 'impaired life' (in the insurance company's terms) for any other reason, such as a heart condition, you may be able to get a better rate.

The table overleaf shows how the rates vary between men and women, people of different ages, and different types. The rates here are the best rates available in that particular week for 'compulsory purchase' annuities, which are those purchased from your fund at the time you start your pension. There is another sort – 'purchased life' – which you can buy with any other sort of capital, and for which the price, and the tax situation (as explained on pages 102–103) is different. The figures below are for the first year's pension, as an annual figure, provided in return for a capital payment of £10,000.

Gender/age	Level annuity, without guarantee	Level annuity, guaranteed for 5 years*	Annuity increasing by 5% a year (no guarantee) - starting rate
Man aged 60	£661.20	£657.60	£370.80
Woman aged 60	£610.80	£609.60	£332.40
Joint life (man aged 60, woman aged 55)	£588.00	£585.60	£301.20

(Source: *The Annuity Bureau – www.annuity-bureau.co.uk –* June 2002)

The guarantee here is that the pension will continue to be paid for a minimum of 5 years, even if the individual dies before that.

Investment-linked annuities

These come in several types, and new varieties are coming onto the market all the time.

Unit-linked annuities

Unit-linked annuities are available from a limited range of insurers. The annual income from this type of annuity depends on the value of the units in the underlying fund, so it can vary considerably. If you are of an optimistic nature, a unit-linked annuity might suit you. In the long term, it could provide an element of growth that is missing from level-rate annuities. But the income fluctuates with the fortunes of the stock market, so you should not expect to be able to rely on it for basic living costs.

With-profits annuities

An even more limited range of companies offer 'with-profits' annuities, sometimes only to existing policyholders. These give a fairly low guaranteed income plus annual bonuses from the with-profits fund. The initial income may be raised by anticipating the annual bonus, but if the bonus turns out to be lower than expected your annual income will also be lower, and vice versa for a bonus that proves to be higher than expected.

Other new types of annuity

One insurance company has an annuity that allows you to change the bonus rate (see above) up to three times – perhaps by becoming more cautious as you get older. Another allows you to buy 'temporary' annuities lasting five years at a time, so that the rates and terms can be changed as you get older. A more recently launched product puts most of the money into the financial markets, so that the income can go up or down, and adds a certain amount of money as you get older (called a 'mortality subsidy' and coming from the funds of those who die before you).

Investment-linked annuities carry risks, but they do allow you to share investment gains if the stock market does well. You could see them as a half-way house between a conventional annuity and the riskier income drawdown (covered on pages 103–105). They are complex products, so it is very important that you take advice, and understand fully what you are going into.

What happens on your death?

If you buy a 'joint-life' annuity, this continues until the death of both parties. This is the type that married couples normally buy. When one of the couple dies, there are a number of variations in what happens next. Check the policy details to be sure you are buying what you want.

With either a single-life or a joint-life policy, you can buy:

- a 'with proportion' annuity, which offers a proportion of the next instalment of the annuity if you die between payments;

- one that guarantees to pay some or all of the payments for a minimum number of years – often either five or ten years – even if you die before this;
- one that makes a payment of the difference between your original outlay and the income so far paid out by the company – called a 'capital-protected' annuity.

Costs

The rule of thumb is that the standard annuity is a level-rate one, covering only a single person and dying with them. You pay more for any additional features in that you have to accept a lower starting income. So you must weigh up their real value to you.

Inland Revenue restrictions

The Inland Revenue imposes some restrictions on the type of annuity you buy:

- If you choose one which gives you an income for a guaranteed period, that period cannot exceed ten years.
- The continuing payments to a surviving spouse or partner must not be larger than the original pension. So, for example, if you buy a pension of £100 a month, you cannot arrange for the surviving spouse to receive a pension of more than that amount.

The Inland Revenue also makes a distinction between two main types of annuity:

A compulsory purchase annuity is bought with the proceeds of an employer's pension scheme or a personal pension. The income from this kind of annuity is taxed as earned income.

A purchased life annuity is bought with your own capital at a time to suit yourself – even though you may be using the lump sum from your pension fund. Part of the income from a purchased life annuity is treated as repayment of capital and therefore untaxed.

The capital element of a purchased life annuity is worked out by reference to prescribed tables of 'actuarial values' drawn up by the Inland Revenue. In essence, the capital element of a yearly instalment is taken to be the amount of the purchase price divided by the number of years equivalent to the purchaser's life expectancy at the beginning of the annuity.

Example

Brian is aged 70. His purchased life annuity costs £20,000 and provides him with a pension for life of £1,780.80 per year. His age gives the policy an actuarial value of £25,027.36. This is the total amount of income Brian will receive from the annuity if he lives the anticipated number of years. The yearly capital element is £1,780.80 x 20,000/25,027.36 or £1,423.08. More simply, you could say that the Inland Revenue expects him to live another 14 years, so if you divide £20,000 by 14 you arrive at the same result. This part of his annuity income is then free of Income Tax.

Income drawdown

It is possible to begin by taking a pension directly out of your fund, and only buy an annuity when you are older, and this is called 'income drawdown', or sometimes 'income withdrawal'. At present, this can only be done until age 75. There has been pressure on the Government to change the rules, including a Private Member's Bill in Parliament, but the Government seems unlikely to concede. There are tight minimum and maximum limits on the amount taken out each year, related to the amount you could have had from an annuity, and also a requirement for a regular review at least every three years.

Most advisers would say that it is not even worth thinking about income drawdown unless you have a pension fund of more than about £200,000, as the charges for managing the investment, and for advice, will eat too far into a smaller fund. There are some campaigners, however, who would regard annuities generally as poor value and claim that income withdrawal is suitable for people with much lower funds, so long as they have other sources of income as well.

A major difference between an annuity and a drawdown arrangement is that with an annuity, you are buying insurance against living too long, whereas with income drawdown you are on your own. With an annuity, you are putting yourself in a group of people (all the annuity holders with that company), some of whom will live only a few years, some of whom will live for many years. Those who die earlier have their funds redistributed among those who live longer, and the annuity rates are set taking account of the fact that this will happen. The older you are, therefore, the higher the annuity rate that you can buy will be. For income drawdown to be worthwhile, therefore, you need to get an investment return high enough each year to beat the increase in the annuity rate you could have had that year, *after* taking account of the extra charges you will have to meet.

To succeed you may need to be involved in riskier investments than you would like. One estimate is that if you are taking the maximum cash allowed each year, you need an investment return of 9.9 per cent. Even if you take only the minimum cash, you still need a return of 5.5 per cent. Few of the funds available have come near to this performance.

A number of providers market income drawdown arrangements now. With some, you are tied into the products (and therefore the investment skills) of one particular provider. With others, called self-invested pension plans (SIPPs) (see page 89), you have more control and can move between investment funds if you feel you could do better elsewhere.

What you should think about

It is unlikely that annuity rates are going to improve much over the next few years at least, so no-one should think of income drawdown as simply a 'temporary parking place' until they can do better from an annuity.

Another motive for many people is that it will mean that they retain the capital in their own possession so that, if they die within a few years, it can go to their family. There is usually a 35 per cent stand-alone tax on this, and in some cases Inheritance Tax will also be payable. Strong though this motive can be, it is worth checking with your potential heirs about whether they feel the same way; they might prefer to see your capital used to provide greater security in your retirement, rather than preserved to pass to them.

Drawdown only makes sense if it is looked at as part of overall financial planning, taking all your capital and income into account. You need other sources of income before income drawdown is a sensible proposition. Otherwise, you could find that a fall in the market leaves you short of money, at a time when your commitments are not reducing.

Age and state of health matter, as does your own attitude to risk, and to the need to keep a close eye on your investments. Some people enjoy checking their portfolio and understanding the finer points of the tax system, while for others it will only make them anxious. The answers to these questions may change as you get older, or your health or that of your spouse deteriorates.

It is *essential* that you get good advice before going into drawdown, and that you do not enter into any arrangements that you do not understand.

If you have several pension policies, or one of the policies that is arranged in 'clusters', an alternative to drawdown may be to delay drawing an annuity from some of them to begin with, if you do not need the money straightaway, and so benefit from increased annuity levels due to your age later. The Inland Revenue has already changed the rules to allow for greater flexibility here.

INCREASING YOUR PENSION

Personal pensions have generous contribution limits, increasing with age, as explained on pages 83–85. Both self-employed people and employees with a personal pension should think about increasing their contributions to a personal pension. The Inland Revenue's carry-back provisions may enable you to pay in more than would normally be allowed in one year (see below).

Employees might also persuade their employer to make a contribution, although not many do so. There can be tax advantages for both employer and employee in doing this. Employer contributions to a retirement benefit scheme (including a personal pension) are not taxable as income to the employee. Nor are NI contributions payable on the amount of the employer's contributions. The employer will also be able to obtain tax relief on contributions as a business expense.

As explained on pages 83–85, the rules here changed in April 2001, so that it is possible to continue paying into your pension even if you are no longer earning.

Carry-back of contributions

You can choose to have a personal pension contribution (or part of it) treated as if paid in the previous tax year, so long as it paid between 6 April and 31 January, and the 'election' is made at or before the time of payment. The contribution is then treated for all tax and limit purposes as though it was paid in the previous tax year.

This is useful if your income was much higher in the previous year, so that you were paying tax at the higher rate, as you can then claim the tax relief at that rate.

Continuing to pay after retirement age

If you have already reached State Pension age, but are continuing to earn or have other sources of income, it is possible to continue paying into a personal pension until you reach the age of 75. You can put in up to 40 per cent of your earnings and receive tax relief, and when you come to draw the pension you will be able to collect a tax-free lump sum as well as an income, so it can be very tax-effective.

However, as the money will only be in the fund for a fairly short time, you need to ensure that the pension contract you sign is suitable, and does not penalise short-stayers.

CHANGES IN YOUR EMPLOYMENT SITUATION

Joining a new employer with a pension scheme

If you start work for a new employer who has an occupational pension scheme, it will usually be best to join it where possible, as explained on pages 69–70.

Since April 2001 it has been possible to join an occupational scheme and put up to £3,600 into a personal pension as well, under certain conditions (except for the very few schemes which are run with personal pension rules, as explained on page 44). The chief considerations for most people now, therefore, are what they can afford, and what the penalties are on stopping or transferring the personal pension.

For a stakeholder pension (explained on pages 92–94) there can be no penalties for starting and stopping payments, but for some non-stakeholder personal pensions there may be a penalty for stopping the contract early. If your personal pension policy has not been running for long, you may find that very little has gone into your fund yet in any case, as your payments have been eaten up by commission and charges. There may also be a continuing annual administration charge, which can eat away quite badly at a paid up pension.

The options where you have a personal pension and do not want to continue paying into it at the same time as belonging to the employer's scheme, are to:

● suspend the contributions and restart them at some future date (there may be a time limit on this);
● make the policy 'paid up', which means that the provider's charges and commission are deducted from your fund, and the rest is left to accrue investment returns until you are able to draw the pension and lump sum; or
● transfer the money from the personal pension policy into your new employer's scheme (if the scheme will accept it).

Of all the options, suspending contributions may be the least financially damaging. Doing this rather than making the policy paid up, if your contract allows you to do so, may result in lower deductions. It may also be possible to convert the personal pension into an FSAVC, but the money you are paying in continued contributions could be better spent in an in-house AVC, where the charges are likely to be much lower. Make sure that before you take up this option, your adviser has studied the details of the in-house AVC and is able to advise you (in writing) that the FSAVC option is the best value for you. A better option may well be to move from the personal pension into a stakeholder pension, possibly with the same provider if you earn less than £30,000 a year. Check with your financial adviser about the terms the provider will offer.

The adviser may be able to negotiate with the insurance company for lower than usual charges, since you are keeping the money within their control. When you take out a personal pension policy, you have by law to be given a Buyer's Guide which gives projected figures for what will be in the fund over the next few years if you want to transfer it. The actual figures may be different if the investment results are different (either better or worse), but this should give you an idea of the size of deductions.

If your policy has been running for a number of years and you have built up a substantial fund, the choice can be more difficult. You may need to negotiate with the pension provider and the new employer (possibly with the help of an actuary) to find the best deal.

None of these considerations applies if you have been paying a series of single premiums without a commitment to making regular payments.

Becoming self-employed

Especially if you are an older person, it will be crucial to keep up pension payments if you become self-employed, if possible up to the maximum the Inland Revenue allows (see pages

83–85), by taking out a personal/stakeholder pension. The cost is not as heavy as you might expect, as you receive full tax relief.

If you are leaving an employer where you belonged to the pension scheme, you will have to decide what to do about your deferred pension entitlement. It tends to be best to leave it in the scheme (especially if it is index-linked, as in public service schemes). You would need a good reason to transfer it elsewhere, as explained on page 67. Setting up a new SIPP (explained on page 89) might be such a reason, but think carefully before putting all your eggs in one basket.

People with broken employment records

You may feel, like many others today, that you have little job security and are likely to go through a series of short-term jobs, periods of self-employment and periods of unemployment during what remains of your working life. If so, it will be doubly important to choose the right sort of personal pension or stakeholder pension policy in order to maximise your income during retirement. The following are some points to think about.

When you take out a pension, you can either sign a contract with the insurance company (or other pension provider) to pay regular premiums over a period of years or you can pay a single premium in one lump sum each year, with no commitment to go back to the same provider in following years. If your employment prospects are uncertain, it will make better sense to buy a single-premium policy each year. If you find the idea of making a large pension payment all at once too daunting, open a building society account and start a standing order to make regular payments to it each month. Then you can pay the whole lot into a pension policy at the end of the year. If you want to make regular premiums, then you will want a policy that does not penalise you for starting and stopping. This would generally mean a stakeholder-type personal pension (explained on pages 92–94).

You can make contributions to a personal pension scheme even during tax years in which you have no 'net relevant earnings'. With non-stakeholder personal pensions, some regular-premium policies impose penalties if there are gaps in contributions, and may even require you to make the policy 'paid up' (see page 108). Alternatively, use single-premium policies and put in as much as the Inland Revenue allows in later years to make up for earlier gaps.

Even if you see no prospect of a career with one employer, you may well have periods of work with employers that have pension schemes, and it would be unfortunate if you had to pass up the opportunity to join (and get the benefit of the employer's contribution) because you were paying into a personal pension.

You could either take out a single-premium personal pension each year when you do not have an employer's pension available to you, or ensure that you have a personal or stakeholder pension policy that makes no charges for starting and stopping contributions. Either way, it will generally be best to join the employer's scheme when you can.

Stopping work

You may become unemployed or want to take early retirement. The contribution limits apply for each tax year, so if you lose your job part of the way through the tax year, you can use the earnings in that year as a figure on which to calculate your pension contribution. It could be worth using part of any redundancy payment or similar lump sum for this purpose.

You can continue paying contributions even if you are not earning – although this change in the tax rules does not solve the problem of whether you will be able to afford them.

If you have bought waiver of premium benefit (explained on page 86), this should safeguard you against being penalised for a gap in contributions if you are committed to paying regular premiums. Otherwise, investigate the alternatives of suspending contributions or making the policy paid up (see page 108) if yours is a non-stakeholder personal pension which may penalise you for either.

If you are 50 or over, you will usually have the option of starting to draw the pension and lump sum from the policy. There will usually be a substantial reduction, however, if this is being paid early, so it may be better to wait if you can afford to. Check the terms of your policy.

Working after State Pension age

You can normally continue contributing to a personal pension, and postpone drawing the benefit, up to the age of 75. As explained on pages 106–107, this can be beneficial in tax terms. Check the pension policy documents, however, to ensure that it is worthwhile.

The rules on 'income drawdown', explained on pages 103–105, could be useful for someone who wants to take partial retirement. Another way of achieving the same end is to buy 'clusters' of personal pension policies. A number of insurance companies will arrange their contracts in this way. You then start to draw on as many as suits you at any one time.

Remember that you can continue to earn and draw a personal pension at the same time. You will have tax deductions from both sources of income, however.

Pensions Issues for Women

In general, women's pay is lower, and they have more gaps in their employment than men, so that their pensions are also lower. At the same time, women's life expectancy is longer than men's. In the past, the rules about the different sorts of pensions were based on the assumption that men were the 'breadwinners' and that women's employment was marginal. Today, there is equality in most areas of pensions, but there are still issues that affect women more than men.

This chapter therefore looks at all the different types of pension, and how they treat issues such as women in divorce, maternity leave, and part-time workers.

STATE PENSIONS

Working part-time

Many women with home responsibilities take up part-time work, often badly paid, and without any pension entitlement from their employer. If you are earning below the Lower Earnings Limit (around the level of the Basic Pension, currently £75), you pay nothing – nor are you building up qualifying years for your Basic Pension. As soon as you earn above that level, you are building up NI entitlement, but you do not now start paying contributions until you reach the Earnings Threshold (£89 this year).

If you qualify for Home Responsibilities Protection (see pages 120–123), you will get this provided that any earnings you have within the tax year are below 52 times the weekly Lower Earnings Limit. If you do not qualify for HRP, then the DWP will send you a statement, about 15–18 months later, telling you how many Class 3 (voluntary) contributions you need to make to turn the year into a qualifying year. You then need to check with your social security office as to whether it is worth your while.

Part-time work and low pay also affect any entitlement you might have to SERPS/S2P: your lifetime average earnings could be lower than for someone who has worked full-time and then taken a career (or other) break.

The State Second Pension (S2P) (see pages 12–14) gives much more to those earning between the Lower Earnings Limit and £10,800 than SERPS did. Someone earning only just above the LEL will be treated as if they are earning £10,800. This could make it worthwhile increasing your hours to bring you above the LEL.

Married women's reduced-rate contributions

Until 1977, married women and widows who worked for an employer, and earned more than the Lower Earnings Limit, could choose to pay reduced-rate National Insurance contributions.

Since 1977, it has not been possible to choose to start paying at this reduced rate. However, women who had already taken up the option before then can continue to do so, unless they have a break in their employment for two or more complete consecutive tax years. The rate is now 3.85 per cent of earnings between the Earnings Threshold and the UEL.

Example

Angela has been paying reduced-rate NI contributions for many years, but she loses her job in May 2000. She will be able to continue to pay the reduced rate if she gets another job at any time before 6 April 2003. But if the gap is longer than that, she will have to pay at the full rate when she goes back to work.

A widow who remarries can continue to pay reduced-rate contributions after her marriage. You should send a certificate of election (CF 383) with your marriage certificate to your social security office. This certificate also allows you to continue to pay reduced-rate contributions if you change jobs.

You cannot, however, continue with reduced-rate contributions if your marriage ends in divorce or annulment. You must then pay full-rate contributions from the date of either decree.

Class 3 voluntary NI contributions (see page 10) cannot be paid to cover the same period during which reduced-rate contributions have been paid. You cannot get Home Responsibilities Protection (see pages 120–123) for any year when you have chosen to pay reduced-rate contributions.

See Inland Revenue leaflets CA 13 (for married women) and CA 09 (for widows).

Reduced-rate NI contributions give you no benefits in your own right. If it is to be worth changing to full-rate contributions, however, you need to be able to build up sufficient 'qualifying years' to give you a worthwhile pension. You will in any case be entitled to the married woman's pension (60 per cent of the full Basic Pension) once your husband draws his pension at or after the age of 65 (depending on his contribution record). So if you are five or more years younger than your husband, it is likely to be worthwhile only if you can build up your pension to more than 60 per cent of the full amount. If the age gap is smaller, or you are older than your husband, it may be worth ensuring that you have some State Pension of your own, even if it is not very much. If your date of birth is later than 6 April 1950, check what age you will be when you are allowed to draw the State Pension before you make the decision (see page 118).

Example

Jean is seven years older than her husband James and pays reduced-rate NI contributions. She paid full-rate contributions for less than ten years before she married, and is therefore not entitled to a pension in her own right. Relying on her husband's NI contribution record, she will be 72 before she can draw a State Pension, and even older if James defers his pension for a few years. Jean needs to get a pension forecast, as described on page 23. This will tell her whether she will be entitled to any State Pension when she reaches 60, and whether starting to pay full-rate contributions will improve her pension position. Jean can then decide whether it is worth starting to pay full-rate contributions, given the pension she will in any case be able to draw on James' contributions. In Jean's case it may well be worth changing to the full rate: even if this brings her only a small pension, she will be able to draw it for at least 12 years before James can draw his pension.

However, there are other reasons why it can be worthwhile to start paying at the full rate:

- Full-rate contributions will enable you to qualify for benefits such as Jobseeker's Allowance and Incapacity Benefit (although there is a time-lag of over two and a half years before you are entitled to these).

- You will be given NI credits for periods of sickness or unemployment.
- You will be able to get Home Responsibilities Protection if you fulfil the other conditions.
- You may be able to pay Class 3 voluntary contributions to cover gaps in your contribution record.
- You may qualify for some S2P even if you do not qualify for a Basic Pension, as the contribution rates are different.

The younger you are now, the more likely it is to be worth making the change. You are less likely to benefit if you are in your 50s, are younger than your husband, and have not paid NI contributions regularly in the past. Ask for advice from your local social security office or Citizens Advice Bureau if you are not sure whether to change to paying full-rate contributions.

Is it worth paying voluntary contributions?

If you would otherwise only qualify for a small Basic Pension in your own right, or you do not have enough qualifying years to get one at all, it may be worth paying voluntary contributions to increase your pension entitlement. If you are a married woman, whether this is worth doing or not will depend largely on whether you are older or younger than your husband. It is more likely to be worthwhile if you are the same age or older than your husband, as with changing from reduced-rate to full-rate contributions (see above).

Women and pension age

Currently, women can start drawing the State Basic Pension at 60, while men have to wait until 65. However, women's pension age is to be increased to 65 in due course. The change is being phased in over ten years, between April 2010 and March 2020. Women born before April 1950 will be unaffected, as they will already have reached 60 before the changeover period starts. Younger women will be able to claim their State Pension at 60 plus an extra month for every month (or part of a month) by which their birth date falls after 5 April 1950. A woman with a birth date of 6 April 1951, for example, will have to wait until she is 61 and one month old, claiming her pension in the year 2012. Any woman born after 6 March 1955 will not be able to draw the State Pension until they are 65. The table below gives the exact dates:

Pension age for women born after April 1950

Date of birth	Pension age (year/month)	Pension date
06.04.50–05.05.50	60.1	06.05.2010
06.05.50–05.06.50	60.2	06.07.2010
06.06.50–05.07.50	60.3	06.09.2010
06.07.50–05.08.50	60.4	06.11.2010
06.08.50–05.09.50	60.5	06.01.2011
06.09.50–05.10.50	60.6	06.03.2011
06.10.50–05.11.50	60.7	06.05.2011
06.11.50–05.12.50	60.8	06.07.2011
06.12.50–05.01.51	60.9	06.09.2011
06.01.51–05.02.51	60.10	06.11.2011
06.02.51–05.03.51	60.11	06.01.2012
06.03.51–05.04.51	61.0	06.03.2012
06.04.51–05.05.51	61.1	06.05.2012
06.05.51–05.06.51	61.2	06.07.2012
06.06.51–05.07.51	61.3	06.09.2012
06.07.51–05.08.51	61.4	06.11.2012
06.08.51–05.09.51	61.5	06.01.2013
06.09.51–05.10.51	61.6	06.03.2013
06.10.51–05.11.51	61.7	06.05.2013
06.11.51–05.12.51	61.8	06.07.2013

Date of birth	Pension age (year/month)	Pension date
06.12.51–05.01.52	61.9	06.09.2013
06.01.52–05.02.52	61.10	06.11.2013
06.02.52–05.03.52	61.11	06.01.2014
06.03.52–05.04.52	62.0	06.03.2014
06.04.52–05.05.52	62.1	06.05.2014
06.05.52–05.06.52	62.2	06.07.2014
06.06.52–05.07.52	62.3	06.09.2014
06.07.52–05.08.52	62.4	06.11.2014
06.08.52–05.09.52	62.5	06.01.2015
06.09.52–05.10.52	62.6	06.03.2015
06.10.52–05.11.52	62.7	06.05.2015
06.11.52–05.12.52	62.8	06.07.2015
06.12.52–05.01.53	62.9	06.09.2015
06.01.53–05.02.53	62.10	06.11.2015
06.02.53–05.03.53	62.11	06.01.2016
06.03.53–05.04.53	63.0	06.03.2016
06.04.53–05.05.53	63.1	06.05.2016
06.05.53–05.06.53	63.2	06.07.2016
06.06.53–05.07.53	63.3	06.09.2016
06.07.53–05.08.53	63.4	06.11.2016
06.08.53–05.09.53	63.5	06.01.2017
06.09.53–05.10.53	63.6	06.03.2017
06.10.53–05.11.53	63.7	06.05.2017
06.11.53–05.12.53	63.8	06.07.2017
06.12.53–05.01.54	63.9	06.09.2017
06.01.54–05.02.54	63.10	06.11.2017

Date of birth	Pension age (year/month)	Pension date
06.02.54–05.03.54	63.11	06.01.2018
06.03.54–05.04.54	64.0	06.03.2018
06.04.54–05.05.54	64.1	06.05.2018
06.05.54–05.06.54	64.2	06.07.2018
06.06.54–05.07.54	64.3	06.09.2018
06.07.54–05.08.54	64.4	06.11.2018
06.08.54–05.09.54	64.5	06.01.2019
06.09.54–05.10.54	64.6	06.03.2019
06.10.54–05.11.54	64.7	06.05.2019
06.11.54–05.12.54	64.8	06.07.2019
06.12.54–05.01.55	64.9	06.09.2019
06.01.55–05.02.55	64.10	06.11.2019
06.02.55–05.03.55	64.11	06.01.2020
06.03.55–05.04.55	65.0	06.03.2020
06.04.55	65.0	06.04.2020

● The State Pension a woman receives, whether based on her own or her husband's contributions, counts as her income for tax purposes. If a husband receives a dependant's increase for his wife, paid with his pension, this will be taxed as part of his income.

Home Responsibilities Protection

Before 1978 a woman (or a man) who stayed at home to bring up children or look after a relative would have had a contribution gap which would result in a reduced Basic Pension. But the system of Home Responsibilities Protection (HRP), introduced in 1978, reduces the number of qualifying years you need in order to qualify for a full Basic Pension.

HRP covers complete tax years only, and does not include any years before 1978. A married woman or widow cannot get HRP for any tax year in which, if she was working, she would only be due to pay reduced-rate NI contributions (see pages 114–117).

You are entitled to HRP if you meet any of the following conditions, or a combination of them, for a whole tax year:

- You are the 'main payee' for Child Benefit for a child under 16. This applies equally to a woman or a man who stays at home to care for children. If it is the man who stays at home, he will need to apply to become the 'main payee' as this is normally the woman.
- You get Income Support and are not required to register for Jobseeker's Allowance because you are looking after someone.
- For at least 35 hours a week you look after someone who receives Attendance Allowance, the middle or higher rate of the care component of Disability Living Allowance, or Constant Attendance Allowance.

For years up to 5 April 1988 you needed to fulfil the third condition for the full tax year, but from 6 April 1988 you must have been caring for at least 48 weeks a year. (If you get Invalid Care Allowance, you will normally be given credits towards your pension instead, as explained on page 11.)

Each year of 'home responsibility' will be taken away from the number of qualifying years you need to get a full pension. But even with HRP you must normally have at least 20 qualifying years to qualify for a full Basic Pension. If you have fewer than this you may be able to get a pension at a reduced rate.

Sheela started work at 16 and paid full-rate NI contributions for 29 years. She then gave up work to look after her mother. Sheela's Basic Pension is worked out as follows:

Working life	44 years
Number of qualifying years normally needed for full pension	39 years
Number of years HRP	15 years
Number of years needed for full pension after taking away HRP years	24 years

As Sheela has the full number of qualifying years, she gets the full Basic Pension.

HRP will be given automatically if you qualify under the first two conditions referred to on the previous page. However, you need to make a claim if you qualify under the third condition, or if you qualify under one condition for part of the tax year and under another for the rest of the year. Ask for claim form CF 411 from the DWP after the end of any tax year when your earnings have not gone above 52 times the weekly Lower Earnings Limit (explained on page 8).

HRP did not cover SERPS pension, but S2P (see pages 12–14) includes credits for carers. This is for a narrower group than for the Basic Pension however. In particular, only children under 6 (rather than 16 as with HRP) qualify a parent for a credit.

● **If you need to claim HRP rather than being awarded it automatically, then for years spent caring between 1978 (when the system started) and April 2002, you can do this at any time up to State Pension age. For years from April 2002, however, you must claim after the end of the relevant tax year, and within three years of the end of it. The DWP computer cannot accept 'running claims', so you need to ensure that you claim for each year that counts. It could be** wiser to make one claim each year after 6 April, rather than save up your claims and send them in every three years.

The DWP computer is also unable to deal with part-years; so you are eligible for HRP only if you have qualified under one condition for a complete year. (For years since April 2002, you even lose HRP for that year if you qualify continuously, but under two separate conditions). So you may need to think about the best time of year to stop doing one thing and start doing another, to maximise your State Pension entitlement.

For information about the new bereavement benefits for widows and widowers, see pages 18–22.

OCCUPATIONAL PENSIONS

Equal treatment

In the past, there used to be considerable discrimination against women in employer-run pension schemes. This has slowly been changing, but there are still many areas where women get a poorer deal than men. Direct discrimination apart, the fact that women's earnings tend to be lower than men's means that they also end up with lower pensions. In money-purchase schemes, women's longer life expectancy means that the 'pot' of money has to last longer, so women receive smaller annuities than men for the same lump sum. European law is still not completely clear about this, but it does look as if such discrimination is permitted.

In 1990 the European Court of Justice took a landmark decision that pensions must be regarded as pay for the purposes of the laws on equal treatment. It was in fact a man who took the case, about one of the areas where men lose out – early retirement (see below). A series of other test cases clarified some of the disputed issues about equality in September 1994. To summarise a rather complex position, it appears that:

- If a scheme has been providing unequal benefits for men and women or unequal pension ages, the 'disadvantaged sex' can claim improvements up to the level of the better-off sex, for service since 17 May 1990.
- However, when the employer changes the rules for future service to bring them into line with equal treatment requirements, they are allowed to reduce benefits for the advantaged sex, to bring them down to the level of the disadvantaged sex.
- European law does not prevent the employer from reducing benefits from pre-1990 past service – but UK employment and trust law will generally do so.
- There are exceptions for actuarially calculated figures, such as early retirement reduction, commutation payments and transfer payments. There are also exceptions where an unequal benefit is there to compensate for unequal State

benefits. In particular, a scheme which provides a 'bridging pension' equivalent to the State Pension is allowed to pay this to men between the ages of 60 and 65 but not to women.

- Part-timers have in the past often been excluded from employers' pension schemes. The European Court of Justice (ECJ) has ruled that this can be indirect discrimination if it affects more women than men and there is no 'objective justification' for it. (See page 127 for details of how the Employment Relations Act 1999 affects this.)
- The ECJ also said that part-timers could claim back service in their scheme, possibly as far back as 1976, although they could be asked to pay arrears of contributions. It left it to national courts to decide on time limits for claims and for back-service entitlement and the House of Lords finally gave its ruling in early 2001, in the *Preston* test cases.

The position now in the UK is that:

- You have up to six months after leaving a job to make a claim that there was indirect discrimination (or you can put in a claim at any time while in that job).
- If you had a series of linked short-term contracts (often called 'umbrella' contracts, and especially common in the education world) the six months only starts to run when the employment relationship ends altogether.

You can claim for arrears right back to 1976, but if you would have been paying contributions during that time, the scheme is entitled to claim these off you in return. However, under UK regulations the employer must pay the whole cost for any service after 31 May 1995.

The process of dealing with these test cases is not over yet, however. More hearings on various points are scheduled for employment tribunals over Summer 2002. Meanwhile, the unions are negotiating with employers who have a large number of cases, such as HSBC and Barclays. This could mean them paying out very large sums of money – £100 million in the case of Barclays Bank – to benefit thousands of women, many of them now retired. The TUC is co-ordinating the unions' response on these, and has said that it is very important that individuals do not try to deal with their cases on their own.

- **If yours is one of the test cases, make sure you consult your union if you receive any correspondence from the Employment Tribunal about it.**

If you are still at work, or have only recently left, there is still an opportunity to put in an Equal Treatment claim if you were discriminated against as a part-timer in the past. Contact your union, or the Office of the Pensions Advisory Service (OPAS) at the address on page 163, before doing so. It may be possible to negotiate a deal on this without needing to go through the legal formalities.

If your employer has altered your pension rights in a way that it is not legally entitled to do, you can put in a claim to have your rights reinstated. You may be able to challenge unfair treatment in future, at any time before the date when you would originally have retired, if you do not want to cause friction with your employer now. Ask the scheme administrator for details of the current position.

Maternity leave

The last thing likely to concern a woman about to have a baby is her pension, but it is worth thinking about. Pregnant women in the UK, regardless of the hours they work or their length of service, must be given 18 weeks' paid maternity leave. During this time their contractual rights, including pension rights, must be maintained. Occupational pension schemes must also make other periods of *paid* maternity leave pensionable, as if the woman was receiving her usual rate of pay.

The law is not completely clear on unpaid maternity leave, but it appears that scheme rules can say that periods of unpaid leave will be credited if the employee pays her share of the contributions, or they can make no provision for this (so long as anyone else on unpaid leave is treated in the same way). But even if the period of leave is not pensionable, you should be treated as having continuous service for the periods on each side of the gap, and not as having left and returned.

Part-time work

Under the Employment Relations Act 1999, part-time employees must not be treated less favourably than full-time staff doing comparable jobs, on pensions as on other issues. This should make challenges to schemes that still prevent part-timers from joining easier, and should lead to the redesign of many schemes.

However, if you work part-time your earnings will be low, which means that your pension from your employer will also be low. In addition, some pension schemes penalise part-timers in the way that the pension is calculated. These are so-called 'integrated' schemes, where the equivalent of the State Basic Pension is deducted from the pensionable salary to start with. This has a relatively greater effect on part-timers with low earnings than on full-time employees who earn more. Try to put pressure on the employer to change this if it applies to you. A recent legal ruling, however, has said that it is legal for the scheme to be designed in this way, even if it does hit women harder than men.

If your earnings are low, you may feel that you cannot afford to join the pension scheme on offer from your employer and that you will be able to rely on your husband's pension. But you can never be sure that your marriage will last and joining the scheme will often add some financial protection in the event of death or ill-health. With the tax relief on contributions, the actual cost of joining the pension scheme in your own right is not high.

On the other hand, women receive the SERPS/S2P pension at the same rate as men, but they are likely to receive it for longer. In money-purchase schemes, the age at which women should stop contracting out (explained on pages 47–49) is therefore lower than that for men. If your earnings are low, a relatively higher proportion may be absorbed by administration costs (although costs should be low in an employer-run scheme), and it may not be sensible for a woman to contract out of S2P on a money-purchase basis at any age.

PERSONAL PENSIONS

Personal pension contributions

Women's career patterns are often disrupted by caring for children and other dependants. Since April 2001, you have been able to pay into a personal pension (including a stakeholder scheme) even if you are not earning, as explained on page 83. However, even with the best of intentions you may find that the family finances are under too much of a strain to allow this. So if you take out a personal pension policy, a stakeholder type will give you maximum flexibility, as there are no penalties on starting or stopping. Alternatively, if you want an old-style personal pension, you would do better to make contributions through a series of single premiums rather than committing yourself to regular premiums.

If you were already paying into a personal pension scheme before the tax rules changed, and want to start a family, or have to take time away from work for other reasons, check what happens if there is a gap in your contributions. Some personal pension providers penalise you heavily, while others are not too concerned.

You may find that waiver of premiums benefit (see page 86) does not apply in cases of maternity or pregnancy-related illnesses. Although this is discriminatory, it is not unlawful under European law because your personal pension is not an employment-related benefit. (But if the employer is contributing towards it, this is a grey area in the law where there might be a challenge sooner or later in the European Court of Justice.)

Contracting out of S2P

Women need to be very cautious about taking out an appropriate personal pension to contract out of S2P. Their longer life expectancy and lower average earnings mean that in general staying with S2P is the better policy.

Annuity rates

As pointed out on page 96, a woman paying over a lump sum to an insurance company will get a smaller annual annuity payment than a man would for the same amount. This appears to be lawful, although once again if the employer has set up the personal pension scheme or is contributing to it, there may be questions under European law.

An annuity bought with the Protected Rights element of an appropriate personal pension does, however, have to be equal for men and women of the same age. But a woman retiring at 60 will receive less than a man at 65.

Stakeholder pensions

Stakeholder pensions have advantages over current personal pensions for anyone with broken employment, because there are no extra charges for stopping and starting payment, or for transferring. However, the 1 per cent of fund charge, explained on page 92, is still quite high, and will continue to eat into the fund whether you are making payments or not. The Government's aim is that people earning below £10,800 (in 2002 earning terms) should stay with S2P, while those earning above that level should contract out (see pages 12–16).

Many women will be earning somewhere around this level. If they work for a public sector employer, such as the National Health Service, they will also be in (or have the chance of joining) a good occupational pension scheme. To avoid this group having to make an impossible choice, there is to be a top-up pension paid by the State, to people earning less than £24,600 and belonging to an occupational scheme. This takes account of the difference between the S2P calculation and the SERPS calculation. So the general advice can still be that you should join your employer's pension scheme if one is available.

PENSIONS AND DIVORCE

The State Basic Pension

There are some special rules which help divorced people who do not qualify for a full pension based on their own contributions, so long as they have not remarried. If you are in this position, you may be able to use your former spouse's contribution record to fill in gaps in your own and to help you qualify for a State Basic Pension. The DWP checks both contribution records when you retire. If your ex-spouse's record will give you a better pension than your own record, they substitute it for yours. They can do this either from the date of the marriage to the date of divorce or from the beginning of your 'working life' up to the date of divorce (or the year before State Pension age in both cases). This makes no difference to the former spouse – it is simply a book-keeping exercise.

Under the 'pension sharing' rules (explained on pages 132–133) it is possible for the SERPS/S2P pension to be divided as part of the divorce settlement, like any other pension. It is rare for judges to order this, however.

If you get divorced before pension age and have been paying contributions at the reduced (married woman's) rate, you will have to transfer to the full rate. If you are divorced after pension age and are receiving the married woman's pension, you may be able to use these rules to get a full pension. In this case, it is the husband's contribution record, up to the year in which you reach pension age, which counts.

People who remarry

If you remarry before pension age, you lose the right to use your former spouse's contribution record for your pension. And if you divorce again, you can only use the last spouse's contribution record in this way. But if you remarry after pension age you do not lose the pension you already have.

See Inland Revenue leaflet CA 10.

> **Example**
>
> **Joan** is divorced after 30 years of marriage. She remarries at the age of 58 to a man five years younger than herself. She has not paid enough NI contributions for a pension in her own right, so she will get a pension only when her second husband qualifies for one at the age of 65.
>
> However, if she had postponed the marriage until she was over 60, she might have been able to get a full Basic Pension based on her former husband's contribution record.

Separated people

Because the marriage is still legally in existence, the arrangements for spouses to make use of each other's contribution record do not apply. But when the husband in a separated couple claims his Retirement Pension, his wife will be able to claim a married woman's pension of £45.20 if she does not qualify for a pension on her own NI record.

If a woman in a separated couple is under 60, her husband will get the dependant's increase for her if he is 'contributing to her maintenance' by paying at least the same rate as the increase (£45.20 in 2002–2003). The rules discriminate against men however: for a woman to get an increase for her husband, she must in addition have been receiving incapacity pension with an increase for him as a dependant, before she went on to Retirement Pension. From 2010 onwards, the rules will be the same for men and women.

Occupational pensions

In the past, it was not possible to divide an occupational pension between a husband and wife who got divorced. The law has changed twice in recent years, however.

Earmarking

Where the divorce process was started after July 1996, it is possible to 'earmark' part of an occupational pension for an ex-spouse. This means that once the pension starts being paid, it is divided between the member and the ex-spouse according to a judge's order. It dies with the member, however, and if the ex-spouse remarries he or she loses it.

Earmarking is complicated and does not work very well, so there have been very few orders made.

Pension sharing

For divorces where the petition was issued after 1 December 2000, 'pension sharing' is now available. This means that an occupational, stakeholder, or personal pension can be divided at the time of divorce, and the ex-spouse will generally then be able to transfer it elsewhere.

Even if the divorce petition was issued before 1 December 2000, it is possible for the other party to issue their own petition and ask the court to 'consolidate' the two, so that the new pension sharing rules apply. It is *essential* that anyone thinking of getting a divorce in a situation where one or other party has substantial pension rights, gets legal assistance. The new rules, and the forms that need filling in to give information to the courts, are complex and it is easy to make mistakes.

Pension sharing means that:

- As part of the information-gathering for the financial settlement, the scheme member will be asked to obtain details of the transfer value (explained on page 65) from the pension scheme.
- The court may make an order that part of this transfer value is passed over to the other spouse.
- Depending on the type of scheme it is, and the policy the trustees have adopted, the other spouse may then have to leave it with the member's scheme for them to look after, transfer it to her own scheme or a personal pension, or have

a choice of doing either. (Information about which options are available in any particular scheme will be included along with the details of the transfer value.)

- The amount that has been passed over to the other spouse is treated as a debit from the original member's pension. If he or she earns less than a certain amount (£24,300 in 2002–2003) the member can put in extra contributions to build what's left back up to the maximum the Inland Revenue allows. For higher earners, however, the 'debit' has to be treated as if it is still part of the pension, when calculating what the maximum is.

Where both spouses are young, or both have roughly equal pensions, the courts are unlikely to make a pension order. It is where one person has a much greater pensions entitlement than the other – a senior civil servant whose wife has been working part-time while looking after young children, for example – that it will apply. Even then, if there are other assets, such as the value of an owner-occupied house or a share portfolio, it is more likely that these will be divided, as it is simpler and clearer.

Personal pensions and the new stakeholder pensions can also be divided. For these, it will mean dividing the money in the fund so that each partner can have their own 'pot' and build up a pension on their own account.

Pension Security

Anyone paying into a pension, of whatever sort, is really taking a leap of faith that there will be something there at the other end, when they are looking for a payment out. But there have been scandals and difficulties in the past. So this chapter looks at the question of security, for all the different types of pension, and at how you can pursue a complaint and get redress if things go wrong.

HOW SECURE ARE YOUR STATE BENEFITS?

If you are entitled to a State benefit, it cannot be taken away unless the law is changed, and the State is not going to go bankrupt or disappear as a private company might. But any Government can change the law, so individual rights can disappear altogether, even retrospectively. Whether they do so or not is a political matter – and so beyond the scope of this book.

If you disagree with a decision

When you receive a decision about a State Pension or benefit you will be given information about what to do if you think the decision is wrong. You can ask for the decision to be looked at again and in most cases you will have the opportunity to take your case to an independent tribunal.

If the decision is not changed you have a further month to appeal. Alternatively you can make an appeal straightaway and in this case you should do so within a month of the original decision.

Appeal using the form attached to leaflet GL 24, giving details of the decision you wish to appeal against and the reasons why you think the decision was wrong. You will be asked if you wish to attend an Appeal Tribunal (a panel of one, two or three people independent of the DWP) and put your case. If you do not write saying you wish to attend, your appeal will be based on the written information you provide. A tribunal may seem rather daunting, but it is far less formal than a court would be. It is always worth attending rather than letting the case be dealt with in your absence. It is also worth getting advice from a local agency, such as a Citizens Advice Bureau, which may be able to represent you at the tribunal, or help you write to the DWP or prepare your case. You can take a friend or relative along to the tribunal if you wish.

If you are still not satisfied, you have a right to make further appeals, right up to the European Court of Justice. But don't try to do this by yourself – you will need a lawyer.

In many cases, you will find that the problem lies in the Act of Parliament and the Regulations, so there will be nothing the DWP officers can do about it. In that case your only redress would be through lobbying your MP for a change in the law. As can be seen from the story of SERPS widows' pensions (see pages 20–21), this can have an effect. So it is always worth complaining if you feel an injustice has been done, rather than simply accepting it.

See social security leaflet GL 24 for further information.

HOW SECURE IS YOUR OCCUPATIONAL PENSION?

Most pension schemes, most of the time, are fairly secure and provide the benefits that their members expect without any problems. However, the Maxwell scandal, and a few others during the recession of the early 1990s, made many people feel far less secure about their pensions than they have done in the past.

Partly to address these problems, in 1995 the Government brought in a new Pensions Act. The major changes resulting from this Act came into force in April 1997. The Occupational Pensions Regulatory Authority (Opra) is now in charge of ensuring that schemes are properly run.

Safeguards for scheme members

The vast majority of pension schemes do appear to be well run and properly safeguarded. The number of scandals that has arisen is really very small as a proportion of the number of schemes in existence (although, of course, there should not be any at all). The protection for scheme members at present lies with:

● the trustees;
● the scheme's auditor and actuary;
● the Occupational Pensions Regulatory Authority (Opra); and
● the Office of the Pensions Advisory Service (OPAS), the Pensions Ombudsman and the courts.

The trustees

The trustees are there because most pension schemes are set up under trust law. This is partly to obtain the tax concessions given to pension schemes that meet Inland Revenue requirements. It also means that the money is held separately from the company's accounts, so it cannot be taken by creditors if the company goes into liquidation, unless there is a surplus after all members have had their entitlement.

Almost anybody can be a trustee of a pension fund – including companies (corporate trustees). Many pension schemes allow some of the trustees to be selected by a ballot of the members, or appointed through the trade unions. The 1995 Pensions Act made it a requirement that at least one-third of the trustees should be member-nominated from 1997, unless the employer or the trustees have persuaded the scheme members not to object to a different arrangement. These rules were scheduled to be strengthened from 2002, so that no scheme could have fewer than one-third nominated by the members. The Government has now postponed this change, because it is reviewing various aspects of pensions, but it is expected to bring it in within the next three years.

The duties of trustees are to act fairly and honestly, with reasonable care and in good faith. Scheme members have a right to know who the trustees of their own fund are and to see the trust deed.

Pension scheme contributions

Legally, employees' contributions have to be passed on to the fund by the 19th of the month after which they were deducted (the same date as for tax and NI payments). Not to do this is an offence. When a pension scheme is wound up, any deficit becomes a debt of the employer. But if the scheme is winding up because the company has gone into liquidation, there will not be enough money available to pay the debts, so this is not very helpful.

If your company becomes insolvent and has failed to hand over employees' payments to the pension fund in the previous 12 months, trustees can make a claim on the Government's Redundancy Fund. The claim cannot total more than 10 per cent of the employees' pay or the amount certified by the actuary as the shortfall in the fund, whichever is the lower. If the scheme is contracted out, the Inland Revenue can also in some cases 'deem' NI contributions to have been paid and reinstate people in SERPS/S2P. Any remaining shortfall is a debt on the insolvent company.

There is a compensation scheme if things go wrong, which is paid for out of a special levy on company pension schemes, to cover cases of fraud or theft.

The auditor and actuary

Most pension schemes have to produce an annual report and audited accounts, and all scheme members have a right to see these. Independent auditors have to check the accounts of the pension fund. In an earnings-related scheme the scheme's actuary has to confirm that, in their opinion, there will be enough in the fund to meet the commitments. Different actuaries can, however, have very different opinions. As they are all based on assumptions about the future, they can turn out to be wrong in practice. But there is now a standardised 'minimum funding requirement' (MFR), although it should be stressed that this is a minimum and it is *not* a test of the scheme's solvency. To be comfortable, the scheme should be financed at well above that level. After complaints from business about the impact of the MFR on their profits, the Government has announced that it is abolishing this and replacing it with a new system, but has given no date for the change yet. In the meantime, it has lengthened the timetable for schemes to bring their funding up to the MFR level. While this has satisfied the employers, it has weakened members' security.

If an employer goes into liquidation and the scheme has to be wound up, then if there is not enough money for everyone the trustees have to pay out benefits in line with a strict priority order. Pensioners come at the top of this list, with current active members nearly at the bottom. This does mean that while people already drawing a pension are usually secure, those in the active category – even if they are only a few weeks off retirement – can lose out badly. The best protection is to have active trustees, and a membership who are interested in what is going on, so that the scheme is unlikely to fall into a state where it is underfunded.

Statements showing the value of each person's pension benefits must be provided on request within two months to any member who asks for one.

When things go wrong

Under the 1995 Pensions Act, every scheme now has to have a formal 'internal disputes procedure' for scheme members and potential members. As the first stage of this procedure, you write to a 'nominated person' (usually the pension manager) about your grievance. This person must reply within two months. If you are still not satisfied, you can go to the trustees (or, in a public service scheme, the relevant government department).

After that, if you still are not satisfied, there is the Office of the Pensions Advisory Service (OPAS) and the Pensions Ombudsman. OPAS is a voluntary body drawing on the good offices of retired and active pensions professionals around the country. It will give advice and take up grievances; it can be contacted directly or via a Citizens Advice Bureau. If you feel that your dispute is especially complex, you may like to ask OPAS to help you go through the disputes procedure.

Many of the cases OPAS deals with are simply the result of misunderstanding and poor administration; these can be cleared up fairly quickly. Those problems it cannot solve are referred to the Pensions Ombudsman for investigation. The Ombudsman can deal with questions of maladministration, or disputes over fact or law, and has the power to enforce decisions through the courts.

The alternative route with a grievance is to go to court. But this is a slow and cumbersome procedure, and there is also the risk of high costs. It is possible for scheme members to get a court order that the fund should pay the costs, but there is always the risk that the court will not agree to it. This is one reason why the Pensions Ombudsman was first set up.

Employment tribunals also play some role in pensions, especially where there is an issue of unfair dismissal or discrimination on grounds of race or sex. They are much cheaper to deal with than courts, although they can still be very legalistic.

If you have a query or complaint about your pension scheme, the first port of call should usually be your union or staff association, if there is one. Otherwise, the local Citizens Advice Bureau should be able to help, and will refer you to OPAS if necessary.

If you think that something is wrong with the administration of the pension scheme, and they might be breaking the law, contact the Occupational Pensions Regulatory Authority (Opra) (at the address on page 163).

For further information see the Opra leaflet *A Problem with your Company Pension?*

Getting information

You have a legal right to information about your company scheme. Ask your union representative to write to the administrator or secretary of your company pension scheme. If you have no union, write on your own behalf.

If the information you request is not given to you, complain to Opra.

The subjects to ask questions about might include, for example:

- Who are the trustees? How often do they meet?
- Do they include member and/or pensioner representatives, or are there outside independent trustees?
- Who manages the pension fund investments and how is performance measured?
- Are the largest investment holdings in well-known companies? Are investments concentrated in a small number of companies?
- Does the fund 'self-invest'? This means investing in the employing company's shares, in loans to the company, or in property occupied by it. Self-investment is now legally limited to 5 per cent of the value of the fund (except for SSASs, as explained on page 52). However, if the investment existed before the law came in, the level may still be being brought down.

Ownership of pension fund assets

Contributions to an employer's pension fund are made by employers and employees, or by employers alone if the scheme is a non-contributory one. Employers tend to assert that if the fund builds up surpluses (see below), those surpluses belong to them and can therefore be used as they wish.

The law is not entirely clear, but it does tend to back up this view. The legal ownership of the pension fund in fact lies with the trustees – that is what they are there for. But control, which is the more important point, is weighted towards the employer.

Surpluses

Pension scheme finances have to be worked out in the long term, as current employees could still be receiving pensions more than half a century ahead. The work of forecasting the amount that needs to go into the fund is done by actuaries. Understandably, their guesswork is often wrong. In the 1980s (less so nowadays) many pension funds for earnings-related schemes were found to have more money than the actuary calculated that they needed. In the case of the largest schemes, surpluses could run into billions of pounds.

Since 1987, the Inland Revenue has required that a special valuation is done every three years, based on rather cautious assumptions. If this shows that the scheme is more than 5 per cent overfunded, a programme for reducing the surplus over a five-year period has to be agreed. This can include:

- increasing pensions for current pensioners or promising more for future pensioners;
- reducing or suspending employer or employee contributions to the fund (known as a 'contributions holiday'); or
- making payments to the employer (in this case the Inland Revenue charges 35 per cent tax).

If none of these things is done, then the surplus element (above the 5 per cent threshold) of the pension fund loses its tax relief.

The rules of most schemes, drawn up before the large surpluses of the 1980s, allow for members to pay a fixed percentage of their earnings and for the employer to pay 'the balance of the cost'. So the employers were legally entitled to say, 'There is no balance of cost – there is more than enough in the fund.' So one common way of reducing a surplus was for the employer to take a 'contributions holiday'. Although legitimate, this is much disliked by members.

In many (but sadly not all) cases, employers 'split the difference' to a certain extent with the members, giving them improved benefits at the same time as making a reduced contribution themselves. One firm still had a surplus after two years of contributions holiday for both employer and employees. This was then used to give a 7.5 per cent increase in pension payments to widows, early retirement at members' request from the age of 62, and improved terms for early retirement on the grounds of ill-health.

If the employer is planning to take a payment out of the fund to reduce a surplus, all scheme members must be given notice, and they can object to Opra if they wish. There is also a 35 per cent tax charge. This means that very few employers take payments out these days, although 'contribution holidays' are quite common.

Mergers and takeovers

If your company merges with or is taken over by another, good practice is to continue with benefits that are at least equivalent to those in the previous scheme. Often this will be a condition of the sale. However, the new company may decide not to set up a pension scheme or to wind up the old one. The trustees then have to buy deferred pensions, based on your length of membership and earnings, from an insurance company. Alternatively, they may set up a money-purchase scheme that offers poorer benefits than your previous one and invite you to transfer your pension into it.

If the new employer is running a scheme at all (even if it is worse than the previous one), it will almost always be worth joining it. Whether you should transfer your previous scheme benefits for the years you were a member there is much more doubtful. If the new employer is financially secure, and you are offered year-for-year credits or something comparable, it could be worth transferring. If you are not sure of the new employer's viability, or think your own job might disappear rather quickly, you probably should not. You should also be very cautious about transferring from a final salary scheme to a money-purchase one. Much depends on your age, your earnings, how good the old scheme is and what the new one offers. Press for the new employer to arrange individual financial counselling, as there is too much variation for blanket advice to be useful.

It is only possible for an employer to make a 'bulk transfer' without the members' consent if the actuary will certify that the members will receive past service benefits in the new scheme as good as those they are giving up. Since it is very difficult to say this, bulk transfers without consent are rare.

Pension rights in a takeover are not protected under European law although this may change. So far as their own staff and those in other parts of the public sector are concerned, there have been directives from the Government about treatment of pensions when work is transferred to private contractors. This means that normally public sector workers' pensions, both past and future, are well-protected. A private sector employer hiving off parts of the workforce should be pressed to do the same.

If your pension scheme is to be wound up, check the trust deeds. There may be a clause which empowers the trustees to use fund surpluses to improve benefits for scheme members before any funds can go to the employer. However, this is often a matter of discretion, and they may come under pressure from the employer to act differently.

HOW SECURE IS YOUR PERSONAL PENSION?

Getting good financial advice

It is a good idea to take advice when buying a personal pension or an annuity, but how do you ensure that you are getting good advice?

Authorisation of financial advisers

Currently, financial advisers must, by law, belong to one of two groups. They must either be the appointed representative of a particular company or be an independent financial adviser (IFA).

Always check which category someone falls into. Their notepaper and business cards should tell you this. An insurance company employee, or an appointed representative, is allowed to tell you only about the company's own products. Most banks and building societies, and many small firms of consultants, are the appointed representatives of specific insurance companies (sometimes called 'tied agents'). Independent financial advisers are supposed to look at all the products on the market and advise about what is suitable for you. Major changes are planned in the way that financial advisers work and it is expected that there will be other sorts of advisers introduced.

The Financial Services Authority (FSA) has a central register that details what kind of business a financial adviser is authorised to do. For more information see the *FSA Guide to Financial Advice*, available free from the FSA at the address on page 162 or on its website. You can call the FSA consumer helpline to check that any particular adviser is properly authorised.

Advisers who are doing their job properly will complete a detailed 'fact-find' – a questionnaire about your financial circumstances. This should include details about your whole financial position, and especially about whether you have an employer's pension scheme open to you. If they do not do this, or if they play it down as 'just a formality', treat them with extreme caution. However, where the employer is making a contribution to a Group Personal Pension, the FSA does allow a 'fast track' procedure without the full fact-find.

For stakeholder pensions, it is expected that in many cases detailed advice will not be necessary. It is not covered by the normal charges for a stakeholder pension, so if you want such advice you may need to pay extra.

Decision trees

To help people decide whether a stakeholder pension would be a good choice for them, the FSA has produced a consumer factsheet containing 'decision trees' for employed people, the self-employed and people who are not employed but who might be able to contribute to a personal pension. It is also available on the FSA's website at www.fsa.gov.uk

The decision trees are in two parts. The introductory notes explain what a stakeholder pension is and how it works. The notes also give details of the State Pension scheme and list some of the questions that you might want to ask. The actual decision trees follow, and include questions about your pension arrangements and circumstances. Answering these will help you think about your pension options. The decision trees give some pension estimates based on your age and how much you can afford to contribute regularly to a stakeholder pension.

If you simply fill in a form for a personal pension or stakeholder pension and send it with a cheque, no extra advice or information will be offered by the provider. So before doing this, read the FSA's factsheet, or take yourself through a decision tree. If you make an enquiry to a provider or an independent financial adviser about taking out a stakeholder pension, the firms selling them will be required by the FSA to make sure that customers have decision trees in front of them when being taken through the process over the telephone. The outcome will have to be confirmed in writing, with a copy of the route taken through the tree included. Where an adviser recommends a traditional personal pension, perhaps a Group Personal Pension, the adviser will need to include in the letter an explanation of why this was considered at least as good an option as a stakeholder pension.

How financial advisers are paid

Most financial advisers work on commission, which means that part of your payment goes to them without ever going to the insurance company or other provider. For regular-premium contracts, there is often an 'initial commission payment' which can eat up much of your first year's premiums – and in some cases also part of the second year's. Taking out all the commission at the beginning is described as 'front end loading'. Many insurance companies, however, have now moved away from this and spread the commission over the lifetime of the policy. It is for you to decide what you want, therefore, and look for an insurer who meets your requirements. For stakeholder pensions, whatever commission the insurance company pays to the adviser, the cost to you can be no more than 1 per cent of the fund per year.

It is also possible to pay your financial adviser an up-front fee instead, and have the amount you would otherwise have paid in commission added back to your premiums or paid to you in cash. The fee could be £200 or more, but it may well be worth it to get unbiased advice. Many advisers will offer the first half hour free.

A list of fee-paid advisers (funded by the advisers themselves) is available from the Money Management Register of Independent Fee-Paid Advisers, tel: 0870 013 1925. The Institute of Financial Planning (address on page 164) also has a national register of fee-based financial planners.

Duties of independent financial advisers

Independent financial advisers are legally supposed to stick to three principles:

Best advice They should find out enough about your personal circumstances to enable them to give advice about what is best for you, regardless of whether it brings them a high level of commission or not.

Best execution Where a product is available at more than one price, they should shop around, find the best bargain, and pass on the savings to you.

Suitability The product must be suitable for your needs.

If you are not satisfied that an independent adviser is fulfilling these duties, you can complain first to the compliance officer within their firm and then to the Financial Ombudsman Service (address on page 162).

Special rules for stakeholder pensions

Currently, the rules are that 'tied' advisers (see page 146) are not allowed to recommend products from other companies. This is called 'polarisation'. The FSA has lifted these restrictions for the sale of stakeholder pensions. This will mean that, for example, a consumer looking to buy a stakeholder pension through a high street bank may be offered not only the bank's own products but also those of other, unconnected, product providers.

How to make sure you get the best advice

You will get the best service from a financial adviser if you already know what you are looking for. Think about whether you should sign a regular premium contract or pay single premiums each year. Ask about:

- charging structure;
- taking earlier or later retirement;
- increasing or decreasing your premiums; and
- what benefit is payable on death.

They will provide you with a buyer's guide giving all their details. Dull as it is likely to be, it will be worth checking through it and questioning anything on which you are not clear.

If you are offered an appropriate personal pension (to contract out of S2P) or if you are being pressed to transfer from your employer's scheme, ask for a specific written statement about why the adviser is recommending this.

Normally, you would make any payment cheque out to the insurance company or other provider, *not* to the financial adviser. Be very cautious if the adviser suggests you pay them.

By law, you are entitled to an annual statement of the value of your personal pension fund and the amount of contributions you have paid in the last 12 months. If the employer is deducting and passing on contributions, the provider should tell the member within 90 days if a payment has not been made within 60 days of the due date. They must also tell Opra (see page 138) within 30 days of a missed payment. Since April 2001 employers are breaking the law if they delay paying over the contributions beyond the 19th of the month following the one in which they were deducted, as with occupational schemes.

Compensation for policyholders

If you have not been given 'best advice' and as a result you have suffered a financial loss, you may be able to obtain compensation from the firm responsible. This has happened, for example, in cases where people have been wrongly transferred out of their employer's pension scheme. It will usually take the form of a payment back to the employer's scheme in return for accepting you back into membership, or as a top-up to a personal pension, rather than cash in hand. There is a system of levies on advisers and financial institutions to cover compensation where firms have gone out of existence.

It is very rare for an insurance company to go into liquidation, but holders of personal pension policies would normally be covered by the Financial Services Compensation Scheme if this happened. Financial advisers and other providers are also generally covered by compensation schemes. In most cases, however, there are upper limits on what can be paid out, so it still pays to take care about selecting your policy.

Mis-selling of personal pensions

There is a major exercise within the pensions world to put right the effects of 'mis-selling' personal pensions in the past. The Financial Services Authority (formerly known as the Securities and Investments Board (SIB)) instructed insurance companies and other providers to check their files, investigate cases where it appears that a personal pension was not the best buy, and take steps – including if necessary the payment of compensation – to put people back in the position they would otherwise have been in.

A number of insurance companies and IFAs, rather than paying compensation, are now offering guarantees that individuals will be no worse off with their personal pension than if they had remained in the employer's scheme. Although any such guarantees must be approved by the FSA, many people are dubious about how strong they will prove to be. Get advice from the manager of your own pension scheme about whether the guarantee is an acceptable alternative to reinstatement.

However, you may have little alternative to accepting the guarantee (or a top-up payment to your personal pension) if your own employer's pension scheme is unwilling to reinstate you. Most larger schemes now have a policy of reinstating people who are still working for that employer, but smaller ones may not, and there is a general reluctance to reinstate people who have since left that job. Check with your employer what the position is, and if necessary press for a change (perhaps via your trade union).

You may have been the victim of bad advice if you were any or all of these things:

- low paid, or with fluctuating and insecure earnings;
- in your 40s or older;
- already a member of an employer's scheme; or
- in a position to be able to join a scheme shortly.

If you are in any doubt, check – and reply to any letters your insurer or financial adviser sends you.

The FSA has set 30 June 2002 as the target date for regulated firms to complete the review into the mis-selling of personal pensions. By then, everyone concerned should have received either an offer of redress or letters explaining that redress is not due. However, there will be some outstanding cases beyond this, particularly with smaller IFAs and those who have gone out of business.

Complaints about personal and stakeholder pensions

The Pensions Ombudsman deals with complaints about maladministration in personal pensions (see address on page 163). The Financial Ombudsman Service (FOS) deals with complaints about the sales and marketing of these products. If you are not sure which you should go to, phone OPAS at the number on page 163, and it will redirect you.

The FOS can help consumers resolve complaints about most personal finance matters. The service is independent, flexible, informal and free for consumers – the address is on page 162.

Consumer publications from the Financial Services Authority

The FSA has a range of guides and factsheets aimed at consumers. These give simple explanations and the information you need to ask the right questions and make informed choices when buying financial products and services. You can order them by phoning the FSA, or if you have access to the Internet, you can also download them from the FSA website at the address on page 162.

Further Information

This part of the book gives a glossary of pension terms and a list of pension organisations that can be approached for further information about pensions. It also has a list of publications from Age Concern Books, information about obtaining Age Concern England factsheets, and an index to help you find your way around the book.

GLOSSARY

This glossary (with the exception of entries marked *, which are additions or amendments) is taken from the Plain English Campaign's A-Z of Pensions, with their permission. It is available on their website at www.plainenglish.co.uk and you can contact them at PO Box 5, New Mills, High Peak SK22 4QP.

Accrual rate In a defined benefit scheme this is the rate at which pension benefits build up for the member. They will get a certain amount for each year of pensionable service.

Actuary An actuary is an expert on pension scheme assets and liabilities, life expectancy and probabilities (the likelihood of things happening) for insurance purposes. An actuary works out whether enough money is being paid into a pension scheme to pay the pensions when they are due.

Actuarial valuation* This is an assessment done, usually every three years, by the actuary to work out what money needs to be put into the scheme in the future, to ensure that the pensions can be paid.

Additional Pension* This is what the Government sometimes calls the pension paid by SERPS/S2P.

Additional Voluntary Contribution (AVC)* This is an extra amount (contribution) a member can pay to their own pension scheme to increase the future pension benefits.

Annuity* This is a fixed or increasing amount of money paid each year until a particular event (such as a death). It might be split into more than one payment, for example monthly payments. Many schemes use an annuity to pay pensions. When someone retires, their pension scheme can make a single payment, usually to an insurance company. This company will then pay an annuity to the member. The money paid to the member is what people usually call their pension.

Annuity rate This compares the size of an annuity (how much it pays each year) with how much it cost to buy.

Appropriate personal pension (APP) * A personal pension approved for contracting out of SERPS/S2P. Rebate-only (or minimum contributions) APPs are those funded only by rebates of NI contributions and tax relief paid over by the Inland Revenue to the pension provider, with no other money going in.

Basic Pension This is what the Government sometimes calls the Basic State Pension.

Basic State Pension This is a pension paid by the Government to people who have enough qualifying years. It is not earnings related.

Beneficiaries These are the people who are paid money, or might be paid in the future, from a pension scheme. For example, there is the individual who is actually paying into the scheme, and also his or her spouse and children who will be paid money if the member should die before they do.

Benefit statement This is a statement of the pension benefits a member has earned. It may also give a prediction of what their final pension might be.

Benefits * With pension schemes, this is everything the member gets after retiring because they were part of the scheme. It usually means the money paid to the member as their pension as well as their retirement lump sum. It could also include death benefits. With insurance, this is the money the insurance firm pays out if something happens. For example, a life assurance policy would pay death benefits if the insured person dies.

Buy-out policy * This is an insurance policy which pension scheme trustees can buy for a member instead of paying them pension benefits. The insurance company will pay the member (or the member's dependants) a pension, either immediately or when it becomes due.

Contracted out This term is used to describe a scheme where the members contract out of SERPS/S2P.

Contributions This is the money paid into a pension fund for a member. It can be paid by a member or an employer.

Deferred pension* This is a pension left in a pension scheme, when someone stops being an active or contributing member.

Defined benefit scheme This is where the rules of the scheme decide how much pension the member will get. There are different ways of working out the size of the pension, but the member will know which system the scheme uses. The most common type of defined benefit scheme is a final salary scheme.

Defined contribution scheme This is where the size of the member's pension is not decided by the rules of the scheme. The size of the member's pension will be affected by how much money is put into the pension fund for the member, how much the pension fund has grown, and what annuity rate is available when the member retires. This system is also called a money-purchase scheme.

Earnings cap* This is a limit on how much of a member's earnings is allowed to be used to work out the limits on contributions and benefits in an approved scheme. This limits the amount that a high earner can put into a pension scheme and still get tax relief.

Earnings-related scheme *See* Salary-related scheme.

Free Standing Additional Voluntary Contributions (FSAVCs)* These are extra contributions that members can pay into arrangements outside their own pension scheme to increase their pensions.

FRS17* This is the 'financial reporting standard' followed by auditors when they decide what figures to give for the cost of pensions in a company's accounts. For a defined-contribution scheme, it is simply the contributions made. For a defined-benefit scheme, the auditor has to decide whether more or less has been paid into the scheme than was needed at the time, and allow for this in the figures that are used. One effect is that if the company gives the workers better pension benefits, the costs will mean that the company's profits are reduced for that year.

Funding* This means setting aside money now, to pay for pensions in the future. The contributions are invested, so that the future income can be added to the fund and increase what is available.

Graduated Pension scheme* This was an additional State pension which was building up before 5 April 1975.

Group Personal Pension (GPP)* This is a system where several employees at one company join a personal pension scheme with the same pension firm. Each member has a separate policy with the pension firm, but contributions are collected together by the employer and passed on.

Guaranteed Minimum Pension (GMP) A member of a contracted-out occupational pension scheme will get at least this much pension unless:

- The member's service is all after 5 April 1997. Their benefits would then come under Limited Price Indexation (LPI).
- Some of the member's service is after 5 April 1997. They would have some of their benefits affected by GMP and some by LPI.
- The scheme is a contracted-out money-purchase scheme. The member's benefits are then affected by Protected Rights.

Home Responsibilities Protection (HRP)* This is the way in which the DWP reduces the number of years in which you have to pay National Insurance contributions in order to get a full pension, if you have spent part of your working life at home looking after children or dependants.

Income drawdown (withdrawal) This is when a member retires, but chooses not to buy an annuity straightaway. Until the member buys an annuity, they take an income from the scheme.

Limited Price Indexation (LPI)* This means that the pension is increased each year by either the Retail Prices Index (the measurement of how prices have risen) or 5 per cent, whichever is the lower.

Lower Earnings Limit (LEL)* This is the least amount someone must earn before they start to build up benefits in the National Insurance system.

Minimum Funding Requirement (MFR)* This is a set of rules, laid down by the Government in the Pensions Act 1995, for how much money a final earnings scheme must have in it to pay for the benefits that have been promised. The calculations are done by the actuary, on the basis of a standardised set of assumptions. The MFR has not worked very well, and the Government plans to abolish it.

Money-purchase scheme This is where the size of the member's pension is worked out by the money-purchase method. The size of the member's pension will be affected by how much money is put into the pension fund for the member, how much the pension fund has grown, and what annuity rate is available when the member retires. This is also called a defined contribution scheme.

National Insurance* This is money that the Government takes from both workers and employers. The amount depends on how much the worker earns. Some Government benefits, such as the Basic State Pension and SERPS/S2P, depend on how much National Insurance you have paid.

Personal pension This is someone's personal pension arrangement. It can also mean a retirement annuity set up before July 1988.

Protected Rights This is the lowest amount of benefits that a contracted-out money-purchase scheme (COMP) can pay to a member. This amount is worked out by using the money-purchase method with the money paid into the scheme as minimum contributions or minimum payments.

Reduced-rate contributions* A lower rate of Class 1 NI contributions paid by many married women and widows. They provide no State benefits in your own right, but only as your husband's dependant.

Salary-related scheme This is a scheme where the member's pension depends on their earnings. It is a type of defined benefit scheme.

Section 32 annuity (also called a Section 32 policy) is another name for a buy-out policy.

Self-invested pension plan (SIPP)* A personal pension where the individual chooses where the money should be invested, rather than leaving the decisions to an insurance company. A SIPP is usually only worthwhile if you have a large amount of money in your pension fund.

SERPS *See* State Earnings-Related Pension.

Small self-administered scheme (SSAS) This is a self-administered occupational pension scheme with no more than 12 members. The scheme will normally be run for a family business. These schemes must meet special conditions, such as having a pensioneer trustee, before they can be approved.

Stakeholder* A stakeholder scheme is a sort of personal pension, which has to meet certain conditions, such as how the scheme is run, and what charges it makes.

State Earnings-Related Pension Scheme (SERPS)* This is the extra State Pension that employed people could earn up to 5 April 2002. They paid extra National Insurance contributions once their earnings reached the Lower Earnings Limit. People could choose to contract out of SERPS by joining an appropriate occupational or personal pension scheme.

State Second Pension (S2P)* This is what the Government replaced the SERPS scheme with in April 2002. It has been designed so that people who do not earn a lot should get a higher pension than they would with SERPS.

Transfer value (TV) This is the amount paid as a transfer payment.

Trustee This is a person or a company appointed to carry out what the scheme must do. They must follow the laws that apply to trusts.

Unit-linked pension In this type of pension scheme the pension scheme benefits depend on what happens to a unitised fund (units in a fund of investments). The scheme is usually linked to the unitised fund through an insurance policy.

Upper Earnings Limit (UEL) This is the highest amount of earnings on which employees pay National Insurance. The employer still pays National Insurance for earnings above this limit.

With-profits policy This is a type of insurance policy. It means that a policyholder will get a share of any surplus in the insurance company's life insurance and pensions business.

Working life* Used to calculate the Basic Pension. It generally lasts from age 16 to just before retirement age. Currently it is 44 years for a woman and 49 for a man but it will be 49 years for both sexes when pension ages are equalised in due course.

PENSION ORGANISATIONS

There are many organisations which are involved in pension activity: reporting, marketing or advising. They include those set up under Acts of Parliament, grant-aided organisations, trade bodies, learned societies and certain professional associations. The following is a list of some of these groups and their functions.

Government bodies and semi-official bodies

Department of Work and Pensions (DWP)

This is the government department which is responsible for paying pensions and benefits. It was reorganised in Spring 2002, and is now divided into 'Jobcentre Plus' for people of working age, and The Pension Service, for all pensions and benefits.

Look on the website www.thepensionservice.gov.uk for information about which office you should contact, or phone the local social security office (in the telephone directory under the old name, the Benefits Agency) for information.

Other useful DWP websites are www.gogetpensions.gov.uk and www.info4pensioners.gov.uk and www.pensionguide.gov.uk

All social security leaflets can be obtained from social security offices or the DWP website (www.dss.gov.uk), and some can be found in post offices too. Alternatively, you can write to:

Pension Guides
Freepost
Bristol BS38 7WA

Pension Service Overseas Branch
Tyneview Park
Whitley Road
Benton
Newcastle Upon Tyne NE98 1BA

Financial Ombudsman Service (FOS)
South Quay Plaza
183 Marsh Wall
London E14 9SR
Tel: 0845 080 1800
Website: www.financial-ombudsman.org.uk
The FOS helps consumers resolve complaints about most personal finance matters. The service is independent, and free to consumers.

Financial Services Authority (FSA)
25 The North Colonnade
Canary Wharf
London E14 5HS
Public enquiries: 0845 606 1234
Website: www.fsa.gov.uk/
An independent body set up by the Government to regulate financial services and protect your rights.

Inland Revenue Savings, Pensions and Share Schemes Division
Yorke House
PO Box 62
Castle Meadow Road
Nottingham NG2 1BG
Tel: 0115 974 1600
Grants tax approval for occupational pension schemes and monitors them to ensure that they do not break the rules for tax relief.

National Insurance Contributions Office (NICO)
Benton Park Road
Longbenton
Newcastle Upon Tyne NE98 1YX
Website: www.inlandrevenue.gov.uk
Deals with National Insurance contribution records and payments. Part of the Inland Revenue.

Occupational Pensions Regulatory Authority (Opra)
Invicta House
Trafalgar Place
Brighton BN1 4DW
Tel: 01273 627600
Website: www.opra.co.uk and www.stakeholder.opra.gov.uk
*Responsible for regulating occupational pension schemes under
the Pensions Act 1995. Actuaries and auditors have a duty (and
anyone else has the power) to 'whistleblow' to Opra if they have
reasonable cause to believe that the trustees or the employer are
breaking the law. Also responsible for registering and supervising
stakeholder schemes.*

Office of the Pensions Advisory Service (OPAS)
11 Belgrave Road
London SW1V 1RB
Tel: 020 7233 8080
Website: www.opas.org.uk
*A voluntary organisation which gives advice and information on
occupational and personal pensions and helps sort out problems.*

Pensions Ombudsman
11 Belgrave Road
London SW1V 1RB
Tel: 020 7834 9144
*Deals with complaints or disputes about occupational and
personal pension schemes. The Ombudsman is appointed by the
Government and is independent of the pension providers.*

Pension Schemes Registry
PO Box 1NN
Newcastle Upon Tyne NE99 1NN
Tel: 0191 225 6316
*Will trace the address of a pension scheme with which you have
lost touch, so that you can find out whether you have a pension
due. Under the control of Opra.*

Trade and professional organisations

Association of Consulting Actuaries
1 Wardrobe Place
London EC4V 5AG
Tel: 020 7248 3163
Professional body for actuaries who work as consultants rather than for insurance companies.

Association of Pension Lawyers
Tel: 020 7667 7216
Website: www.apl.org.uk
An organisation for lawyers who work on pensions.

Faculty of Actuaries
MacLawrin House
18 Dublin Street
Edinburgh EH1 3PP
Tel: 0131 240 1300
Professional body for actuaries in Scotland.

Institute of Actuaries
Staple Inn Hall
High Holborn
London WC1V 7QJ
Tel: 020 7632 2100
Website: www.actuaries.org.uk/
Professional body for actuaries in England and Wales.

Institute of Financial Planning
Whitefriars Centre
Lewins Mead
Bristol BS1 2NT
Tel: 0117 945 2470
Website: www.financialplanning.org.uk
Has a national register of fee-based financial planners.

National Association of Pension Funds (NAPF)
NIOC House
4 Victoria Street
London SW1H 0NE
Tel: 020 7808 1300
Website: www.napf.co.uk/index.html
Members are drawn from the larger occupational pension funds and their advisers. NAPF provides an annual survey of statistics relating to pensions and allied topics and advises its members on what it considers good practice.

Pensions Management Institute
4–10 Artillery Lane
London E1 7LS
Tel: 020 7247 1452
Website: www.pensions-pmi.org.uk
Aims to promote high professional standards in the pensions industry; the major examining board for pension qualifications.

Society of Pension Consultants
St Bartholomew House
92 Fleet Street
London EC4Y 1DG
Tel: 020 7353 1688
Consists of financial advisers, actuaries, and pensions and investment management consultants; acts as a lobbying platform for its members.

ABOUT AGE CONCERN

The Pensions Handbook: Planning ahead to boost retirement income is one of a wide range of publications produced by Age Concern England, the National Council on Ageing. Age Concern works on behalf of all older people and believes later life should be fulfilling and enjoyable. For too many this is impossible. As the leading charitable movement in the UK concerned with ageing and older people, Age Concern finds effective ways to change that situation.

Where possible, we enable older people to solve problems themselves, providing as much or as little support as they need. A network of local Age Concerns, supported by many thousands of volunteers, provides community-based services such as lunch clubs, day centres and home visiting.

Nationally, we take a lead role in campaigning, parliamentary work, policy analysis, research, specialist information and advice provision, and publishing. Innovative programmes promote healthier lifestyles and provide older people with opportunites to give the experience of a lifetime back to their communities.

Age Concern is dependent on donations, covenants and legacies.

Age Concern England
1268 London Road
London SW16 4ER
Tel: 020 8765 7200
Fax: 020 8765 7211

Age Concern Cymru
4th Floor
1 Cathedral Road
Cardiff CF11 9SD
Tel: 029 2037 1566
Fax: 029 2239 9562

Age Concern Scotland
113 Rose Street
Edinburgh EH2 3DT
Tel: 0131 220 3345
Fax: 0131 220 2779

Age Concern Northern Ireland
3 Lower Crescent
Belfast BT7 1NR
Tel: 028 9024 5729
Fax: 028 9023 5497

PUBLICATIONS FROM AGE CONCERN BOOKS

Your Rights 2002–2003: A guide to money benefits for older people
Sally West

A highly acclaimed annual guide to the State benefits available to older people. Contains current information on Jobseeker's Allowance, Incapacity Benefit, Income Support, Housing Benefit and Retirement Pensions, among other matters, and includes advice on how to claim them.

£4.75   0-86242-351-1

Your Taxes and Savings 2002–2003: A guide for older people
Paul Lewis

Explains how the tax system affects older people over retirement age, including how to avoid paying more than necessary. The information about savings and investments covers the wide range of opportunities now available.

£5.99   0-86242-352-X

Changing Direction: Employment options in mid-life: 2nd edition
Sue Ward

The new edition of this topical and highly practical book is designed to help those aged 40–55 get back to work. It helps readers understand their own skills, shows how to look for a job and guides readers through the many positive steps which can be taken. It looks at issues such as:

- adjusting to change
- opportunities for work
- working for yourself
- retraining and education
- age discrimination
- finances.

Complete with a range of personal accounts, this book is a first point of reference for those in mid-life keen to take control of their working lives again.

£9.99   0–86242–331–7

If you would like to order any of these titles, please write to the address below, enclosing a cheque or money order for the appropriate amount (plus £1.95 p&p) made payable to Age Concern England. Credit card orders may be made on 0870 44 22 044 (individuals) or 0870 44 22 120 (AC federation, other organisations and institutions). Fax: 01626 323318.

Age Concern Books
PO Box 232
Newton Abbot
Devon TQ12 4XQ

Age Concern Information Line/Factsheets subscription

Age Concern produces more than 45 comprehensive factsheets designed to answer many of the questions older people (or those advising them) may have. These include money and benefits, health, community care, leisure and education, and housing. For up to five free factsheets, telephone: 0800 00 99 66 (7am–7pm, seven days a week, every day of the year). Alternatively you may prefer to write to Age Concern, FREEPOST (SWB 30375), ASHBURTON, Devon TQ13 7ZZ.

For professionals working with older people, the factsheets are available on an annual subscription service, which includes updates throughout the year. For further details and costs of the subscription, please write to Age Concern at the above Freepost address.

INDEX